BestMasters

Springer awards „BestMasters“ to the best master’s theses which have been completed at renowned Universities in Germany, Austria, and Switzerland.
The studies received highest marks and were recommended for publication by supervisors. They address current issues from various fields of research in natural sciences, psychology, technology, and economics.
The series addresses practitioners as well as scientists and, in particular, offers guidance for early stage researchers.

More information about this series at http://www.springer.com/series/13198

Emil Kraft

Analysis and Modelling of the French Capacity Mechanism

Impact Assessment of Energy Policy Measures on the Security of Supply

With a foreword by Prof. Dr. Wolf Fichtner

Springer Gabler

Emil Kraft
Karlsruhe, Germany

BestMasters
ISBN 978-3-658-20092-3 ISBN 978-3-658-20093-0 (eBook)
https://doi.org/10.1007/978-3-658-20093-0

Library of Congress Control Number: 2017958028

Springer Gabler

Printed on acid-free paper

This Springer Gabler imprint is published by Springer Nature
The registered company is Springer Fachmedien Wiesbaden GmbH
The registered company address is: Abraham-Lincoln-Str. 46, 65189 Wiesbaden, Germany

Acknowledgements

This master thesis was prepared in cooperation with the University Paris Dauphine. Special thanks are due to Jan Horst Keppler (University Paris Dauphine), Marie Petitet (EDF) and Olivier Houvenagel (RTE) for the hospitability during my stay in Paris and the support in the preparation of my master thesis.

Further, I want to thank Wolf Fichtner, Dogan Keles and Florian Zimmermann for the supervision of my work. The chair for energy economics and particularly the research group "Energy Markets and Energy System Analysis" provided an enjoyable and prolific working atmosphere in Karlsruhe and gave me the opportunity to go to Paris for an academic exchange. Being always available for advice, they gave me trust and sufficient freedom to prepare this work according to my own ideas.

Finally, I want to especially thank my family and my friends, who supported me throughout my entire studies and make my life worth living at all times. My parents Ingrid and Dieter, who taught me not only working ethic, but provided me a value compass throughout my entire life. My brother Hagen, who shows me that blood is thicker than water and will always support me in any way he is able to.

Vielen Dank!

Emil Kraft

Karlsruhe, May 2017

Foreword

The present work was prepared by Emil Kraft in the course of his studies in "Industrial Engineering and Management" at the Karlsruhe Institute of Technology and submitted on 30 May 2017 to the Chair of Energy Economics. Mr Kraft has put great effort into his master's thesis, including a stay at the University Paris-Dauphine and exchanging views with experts from RTE and EDF in Paris. This is one of the reasons why the work is convincing, both in terms of its disciplinary and interdisciplinary nature.

Mr Kraft has taken on a very important and topical issue for the efficient organisation of the future European electricity system, namely the analysis and modelling of the newly introduced capacity mechanism in France. In particular, the master's thesis attaches great importance to the economically and politically highly relevant and methodologically challenging topic of analysing the effects of the new market segment on future investment decisions and security of supply. In order to measure the development of the French electricity system, Mr Kraft operationalises the energy policy objectives of economic efficiency and security of supply.

In order to model the capacity mechanism as a supplement to the existing market structures, numerous further developments of the agent-based power market simulation model PowerACE were required, which is used to map short-term and long-term individual decisions at actor level and thus simulate emergent behaviour at system level. The work is impressive due to the level of detail of the modelling with regard to the regulatory framework and the methodology employed by the author with regard to the market logic in a capacity market. Unlike other publications dealing with this subject, Mr Kraft has done both detailed modelling and applied the developed methodology to real French data. This makes the work unique in the scientific context.

In addition to the thorough and detailed methodology, the work convinces by a critical reflection of the simulation results taking into account the energy policy and regulatory conditions in the French market area. Further, the interactions and dependencies between the electricity and capacity market are described in detail.

In summary, I can strongly recommend this work to anyone interested in current and future energy markets as well as the French electricity system, regardless of having an academic or application-oriented background.

Professor Wolf Fichtner

Institute for Industrial Production (IIP), Chair of Energy Economics

Karlsruhe Institute of Technology (KIT)

Table of Content

Acknowledgements .... **v**

Foreword by Prof. Wolf Fichtner .... **vii**

Table of Content .... **ix**

List of Figures .... **xi**

List of Tables .... **xiii**

Abstract .... **xv**

Zusammenfassung .... **xvii**

1. **Introduction** **1**

2. **Overview French Electricity System** **3**

   2.1. Supply Side 3

   2.2. Demand Side 7

   2.3. France in the European Context 11

   2.4. Justification for a Capacity Remuneration Mechanism 12

3. **Decentralised Capacity Mechanism** **17**

   3.1. A market-wide quantity-based Mechanism 17

   3.2. Presentation of Regulatory Framework 19

   3.3. Revisions requested by European Commission 36

   3.4. First Market Results 39

4. **Modelling a Decentralised Capacity Market 41**

4.1. Presentation of Agent-based Simulation Model PowerACE...... 41

4.2. Necessity of a Capacity Mechanism in PowerACE 45

4.3. System Boundaries and Input Data 49

4.4. Logic and Implementation of the Capacity Mechanism Model.. 50

4.5. State of the Art and own Contribution...................................... 70

5. **Results and Sensitivity Analyses 93**

5.1. Reference Case 95

5.2. SoS+ Case.. 102

5.3. SoS- Case 104

6. **Critical Reflection and Outlook.. 109**

6.1. Determination of Mechanism Parameters 109

6.2. Security of Supply Evaluation.. 112

6.3. Demand Adaption... 112

6.4. Cross-Border Participation and Market Coupling 113

6.5. Nuclear Power Plants 114

6.6. Diversification of Bidding Strategies 116

7. **Conclusions 119**

List of References 123

List of Figures

Figure 1: Installed nuclear capacity in France assuming a technical lifetime of 50 years 4

Figure 2: Installed Capacity in France 2016 and French Electricity Mix of 2015 5

Figure 3: Targets for hydro, wind and photovoltaic power of SRCAE until 2020 7

Figure 4: Seasonality of French electricity consumption under smoothed temperatures by use 8

Figure 5: Determination and development of the heating gradient in 1996 and 2012 9

Figure 6: Evolution of the French peak load, effect of electrical heating 10

Figure 7: General logic of the decentralised capacity mechanism 18

Figure 8: Calendrical structure of the capacity mechanism 31

Figure 9: Payments for imbalance settlements, assuming a market reference price of 10,000 € per MW 34

Figure 10: Determination of initial reference price for new investments 39

Figure 11: Demand and supply curve of first capacity auction of 15 December 2016 40

Figure 12: Schematic illustration of PowerACE structure 43

Figure 13: Spot prices of France and Germany in the period of the cold wave 1 till 13 February 2012 47

Figure 14: Logical structure of capacity market model........ 55

Figure 15: Coal, CGGT and peak capacities in the 2030 equilibrium park, with or without a capacity mechanism in France 73

Figure 16: Additional available capacity installed (in comparison to energy-only market scenario) 78

Figure 17: Capacity price development 2017-2040. 79

Figure 18: Left: Capacity price evolution with model-endogenous plant shutdowns, security of supply target 0.5 and 3 hours LOLE and no risk aversion of investor. Right: Capacity price evolution with exogenous plant shutdowns, security of supply target 3 hours LOLE and no risk aversion of investor 85

Figure 19: Capacity price development 2020-2050 90

Figure 20: Capacity price development in the reference case. 96

Figure 21: New investments in the reference case. 97

Figure 22: Capacity price development in the reference case without respecting the price cap. 100

Figure 23: Capacity price development in the SoS+ case. 102

Figure 24: New investments in the SoS+ case. 104

Figure 25: Capacity price development in the SoS- case. 105

Figure 26: New investments in the SoS- case. 106

List of Tables

Table 1: NTC values in winter months 2016 11

Table 2: Reference temperature values for 2017-2020. 21

Table 3: Capacity credits for relevant technologies 24

Table 4: Acceptability margins for relevant technologies. 24

Table 5: Values of the infra-daily availability factor Kh 26

Table 6: Values of the intra-daily availability factor Kj 27

Table 7: Controllability factors for relevant technologies. 27

Table 8: Techno-economic parameters of investment options. 50

Table 9: Results for model park evolution with endogenous shutdown decisions for the energy-only market with a 3,000€/MWh price cap and the capacity mechanism with a 3 hours LOLE target (left), and exogenous shutdown decisions for the same cases (right) 87

Table 10: Experimental design. 94

Abstract

The French electricity system became increasingly vulnerable to extreme weather events in the last years, mainly driven by the strong temperature-sensitivity of the load and insufficient peak load generation. To mitigate the imminent risk to the security of supply, the French government implemented a capacity remuneration mechanism to complement the electricity markets. The present work analyses the capacity mechanism design and develops a capacity market model based on the agent-based power market simulation model PowerACE. Applying the model to real data, the impact of the mechanism on the development of the French generation fleet until 2050 and the evolution of the capacity prices are assessed. Depending on the set security of supply target, until 2028 between 11.9 GW and 17.0 GW of gas-fired power plants are commissioned. The capacity prices are volatile throughout the simulation horizon, mainly driven by the expected generation change in nuclear energy. The key conclusions consist of the effectiveness and the controllability of the implemented mechanism. The capacity mechanism as a complement to functioning electricity markets is able to provide sufficient investment incentives and thus to guarantee the French security of supply in the future.

Zusammenfassung

Die starke Temperatursensitivität der Last und fehlende Spitzenlasterzeugung führten in den vergangenen Jahren zu einer zunehmenden Verwundbarkeit des französischen Stromsystems hinsichtlich extremer Wetterereignisse. Um die drohende Gefahr für die Versorgungssicherheit zu verringern, hat die französische Regierung in Ergänzung zu den Strommärkten einen Kapazitätsmechanismus implementiert. Die vorliegende Arbeit analysiert das gewählte Mechanismusdesign und entwickelt ein Kapazitätsmarktmodell, das auf dem agenten-basierten Strommarktmodell PowerACE basiert. Durch Anwendung des Modells auf echte Daten werden die Entwicklung des französischen Kraftwerksparks bis 2050 sowie die Entwicklung der Kapazitätspreise untersucht. Abhängig vom definierten Versorgungssicherheitsziel werden bis 2028 zwischen 11.9 GW und 17.0 GW an gasbefeuerten Kraftwerken zugebaut. Die Kapazitätspreise weisen eine große Volatilität über den Simulationshorizont auf, die hauptsächlich durch den erwarteten Generationenwechsel in der Kernenergie ausgelöst wird. Die wesentlichen Schlussfolgerungen der Arbeit sind die Effektivität und die Steuerbarkeit des eingeführten Kapazitätsmechanismus. Ergänzend zu funktionierenden Strommärkten ist der französische Kapazitätsmechanismus in der Lage, ausreichende Investitionsanreize zu liefern und somit die Versorgungssicherheit in Frankreich zukünftig zu gewährleisten.

1. Introduction

In the past years, the French electricity system has undergone substantial changes. The paradigm of market liberalisation led to a move away from the traditional monopoly structure towards a competitive market structure. In the same period, the French load properties changed and mainly driven by electrical heating and the consequent temperature sensitivity, the French peak load increased and became more volatile. In combination with the expansion of renewable energy sources in Europe, particularly in the neighbouring Germany, the uncertainty in the French electricity system increased throughout the past decade. In the current market conditions, revenues for conventional generation capacities are not sufficient to foster new investments, especially in peak generation units. As a consequence, the French government decided to implement a decentralised capacity remuneration mechanism to mitigate the imminent threat to the security of supply. The mechanism shall provide appropriate investment incentives for both demand response measures and new peak generation units. It shall reduce the uncertainty for investors by providing an additional source of income to generation units and demand response capacities.

The research questions that arise in this context are whether the capacity mechanism is able to guarantee the French security of supply and what are the mechanism's impacts on the development of the French generation fleet. To address this research questions appropriately, the present work analyses the French capacity mechanism and further develops the agent-based simulation model PowerACE. Applying this model to real data, the development of the French generation fleet until 2050 is simulated and conclusions are drawn.

The present work is structured as follows. Subsequent to the introduction, chapter 2 provides an overview over the French electricity system and a discussion of the security of supply problem. In chapter 3 the regulatory framework of the capacity mechanism is presented and analysed in detail.

In chapter 4 the developed model and the implementation is described, followed by a discussion and reflection over other approaches to analyse the French capacity mechanism. Chapter 5 provides the results obtained from the simulation model and discusses the key sensitivities of the capacity mechanism and the simulation model. In the subsequent chapter 0 the shortcomings of the simulation model are critically reflected and further research requirements are identified. In the end, the work is summarised and the main conclusions are presented.

2. Overview French Electricity System

In order to be able to analyse the French capacity mechanism, a view on the context in which it was implemented is required. For this purpose, the electricity system of France is presented to point out essential characteristics, interactions and interdependencies. Firstly, the supply side is investigated, followed by the demand side. In a second step, possible future issues for the short-term security of supply and the long-term generation adequacy are identified, leading to the justification for the implementation of a capacity remuneration mechanism in France.

2.1. Supply Side

Like in many other European countries, the electricity supply in France was considered a natural monopoly for a long time. Thus, historically the electricity system was organized in a monopoly structure and regulated by the state. The monopolist EDF (Electricité de France) operated the generation and transmission system in France for several decades. In the course of the liberalisation of the energy markets, EDF was decoupled and vertically divested, to guarantee competitive markets and to avoid market distortions. In 2000, RTE (Réseau de transport d'électricité) was founded as the French transmission system operator (RTE 2017a). However, despite being organizationally decoupled and part of a liberalised energy market, the strong structural links between the French state, EDF and RTE remain until today. The French state holds 83.1 percent of the shares in EDF (EDF 2017), EDF holds 50.1 percent of the shares in RTE (CNP 2016). Thus, it can be concluded that the traces of the past remain until today.

The today installed production capacities in France too show a strong mark of the past market system. Considering nuclear energy as the mean to provide cheap and safe baseload electricity to the French population and economy, many nuclear power plants were commissioned by EDF in the 1970s and 1980s, to satisfy the growing electricity demand of France. Between 1976 and 1988, almost 50 GW of nuclear power plants were commissioned by EDF (Platts 2017), being the most important part of France's electricity supply until today. In total, there are 63.3 GW of nuclear power plants by today, operated by EDF (RTE 2017b). However, the rapid expansion of nuclear energy in the past leads to substantial challenges for the future energy system, since from 2026 on within fifteen years more than 50 GW of nuclear energy will become older than 50 years. Thus, major new investments or overhauls to extend the lifetime will be required in the future. Zimmermann et al. (2017) illustrate the imminent investment and overhaul requirements using an hypothetical lifetime of 50 years for nuclear power plants (see Figure 1).

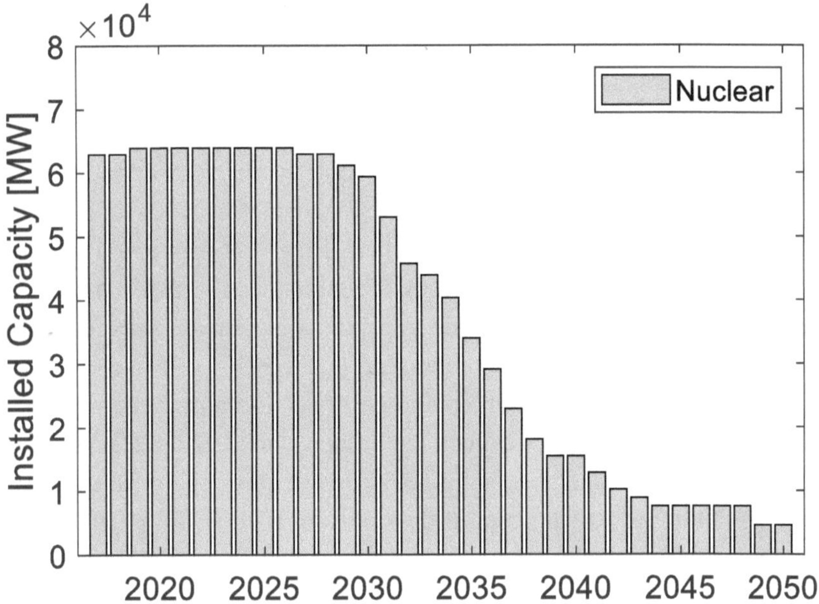

Figure 1: Installed nuclear capacity in France assuming a technical lifetime of 50 years (adapted from Zimmermann et al. 2017).

The installed generation capacity in France and the electricity mix are shown in Figure 2 below. In 2016, the nuclear generation capacity of more than 63 GW makes the major share of the installed capacity and contributes to the electricity mix to more than 75 percent. The second largest installed capacity comes from hydro power with 25 GW. Non-hydro renewable energies and fuel-fired thermal power plants have a minor share in the installed capacity. All fuel-fired thermal plants combined amount to roughly 20 GW, from which a large share are oil-fired or decentral generation units. The share of fuel-fired technologies in the electricity mix is very low compared to Germany, only amounting to less than seven percent.

Conclusively, the French electricity system shows clear traces of the past. The dominant market position of EDF as the former monopoly company is still outstanding, as well as the nuclear share in the electricity provision. Even if French energy markets are organised as a liberalised energy market today, the entire energy supply relies essentially on EDF and its nuclear power fleet.

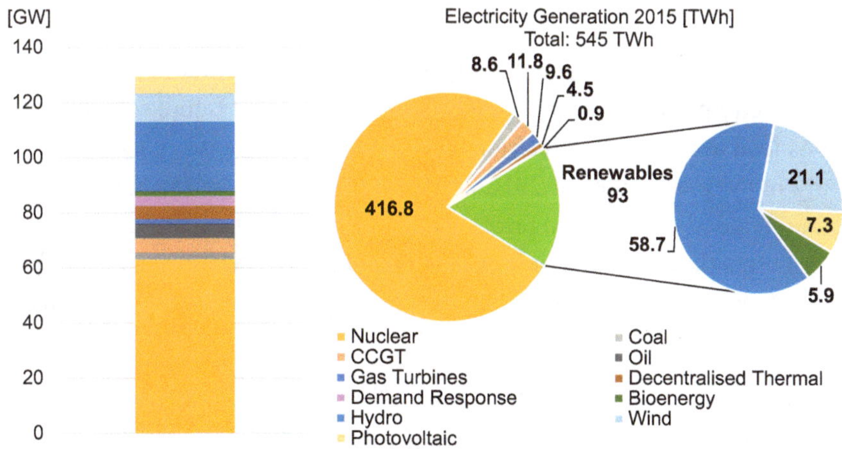

Figure 2: Installed Capacity in France 2016 and French Electricity Mix of 2015 (adapted from RTE 2017b).

To avoid an abuse of the market power and to generate a level playground for competition on the retail market, EDF is obliged to offer a share of its nuclear electricity to market competitors to same economic conditions. The ARENH (accès régulé à l'électricité nucleaire historique, French for: regulated access to historical nuclear energy) scheme, which was introduced by the NOME (nouvelle organisation du marché de l'électricité, French for: new organisation of the electricity market) law in 2010, states that retail companies can buy base-load bands from nuclear energy from EDF according to the load of their connected end consumers at a regulated price. The total volume of the ARENH electricity is capped at 100 TWh, thus roughly a quarter of the total nuclear electricity generation. The price is regulated by CRE (Commission de regulation de l'énergie) and published. Consequently, instead of buying on the spot market, retailers can buy nuclear energy directly from EDF. However, the price, which was determined to 42 € per MWh was more expensive than spot market prices for baseload recently. Thus, the regime was hardly used by any market player.

Nevertheless, for two reasons ARENH electricity is gaining importance again. Firstly, ARENH electricity is also accompanied with the respective capacity certificates, making it more attractive as additional revenues from the capacity market are generated. Secondly, expected future scarcity situations lead to increasing electricity prices on the wholesale markets. Especially in the past winter of 2016/2017, when several nuclear power plants had unplanned outages and prices were forecasted to be high the period of peak demand, many suppliers decided to buy ARENH electricity to decrease their risk, expecting high and volatile prices on the wholesale market.

The future development of the French electricity system's supply side is characterised by a strong expansion of renewable energies. According to SRCAE (schémas régionaux du climat, de l'air et de l'énergie), the government regional development plan for renewable energies until 2020, especially wind and photovoltaic capacities will increase substantially (Figure 3).

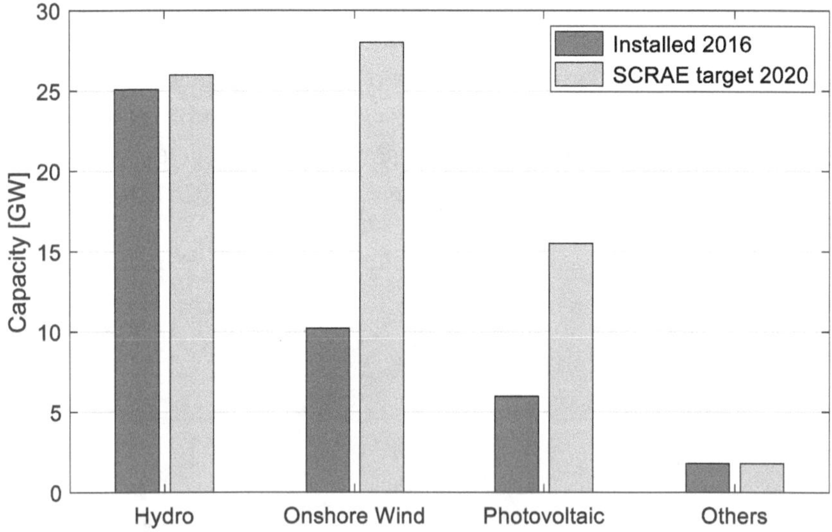

Figure 3: Targets for hydro, wind and photovoltaic power (left to right) of SRCAE until 2020 (own illustration based on RTE 2017b).

The renewable generation shall replace nuclear generation. As stated in the Green Growth Act of 2015, the share of renewable energies in the French electricity mix shall increase from currently 17 percent to 40 percent in 2030. Parallel, the installed nuclear capacity must not exceed the current 63.3 GW and the share of nuclear generation in the electricity mix shall decrease to 50 percent until 2025 (MEEM 2015). Whether and how these target will be met remains to be seen in the future.

2.2. Demand Side

The French electricity consumption in 2015 amounted to 479 TWh. With 34 percent, the residential sector has the largest share in the overall consumption, followed by the tertiary sector with 29 percent and the industrial sector with 24 percent. Agriculture, energy and transport contribute with the remaining 13 percent. (RTE 2017b)

The characteristics of the French demand, that are particularly important for the present work, are the strong seasonality and the temperature-sensitivity of the French load, which is mainly caused by heating use in the residential and the tertiary sector. As shown in Figure 4, the French load during summer is expected to be below 50 GW, whereas it increases strongly in the winter months. In winter, depending on the outside temperature the heating load can vary between 5 GW and 45 GW (RTE 2017b).

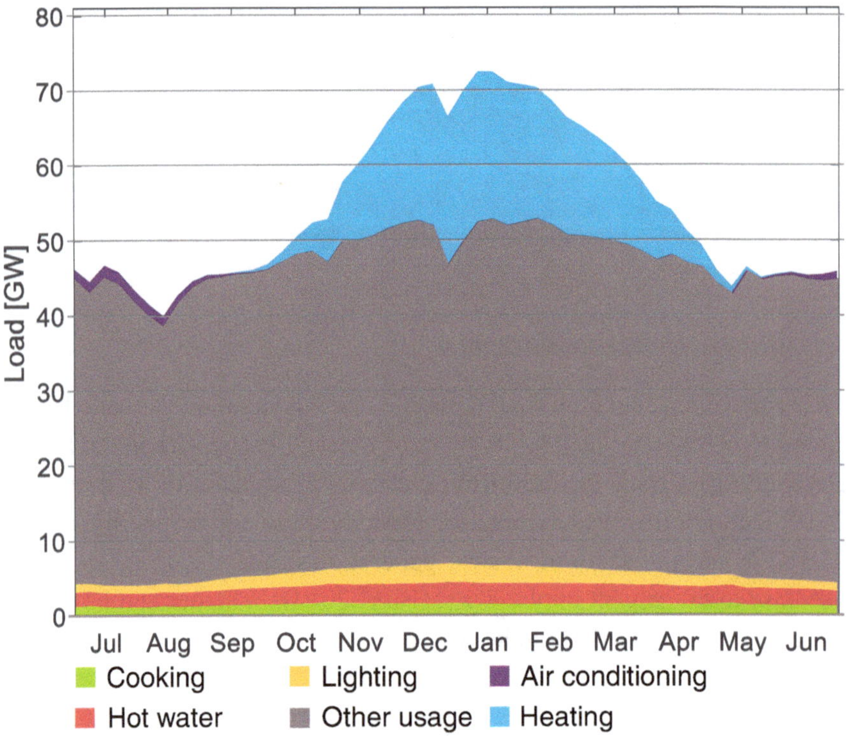

Figure 4: Seasonality of French electricity consumption in GW under smoothed temperatures by use (adapted from RTE 2017b).

The temperature sensitivity is illustrated in Figure 5. The figure shows the average load of each day of the considered year on the vertical axis and the average temperature on the horizontal axis. Applying linear regression on all observations with an average temperature below 15 degrees, the temperature gradient for the year is calculated. For 2012, the temperature gradient was determined to -2.4 GW per degree, in comparison to 1996 both the overall load level and the temperature sensitivity increased significantly. RTE identified an increased deployment of electrical heating throughout the last decades as the driver for the increased temperature sensitivity. Thus, especially during extreme cold waves, the French load is strongly increased for many consecutive days and causes scarcity situations in the French electricity system.

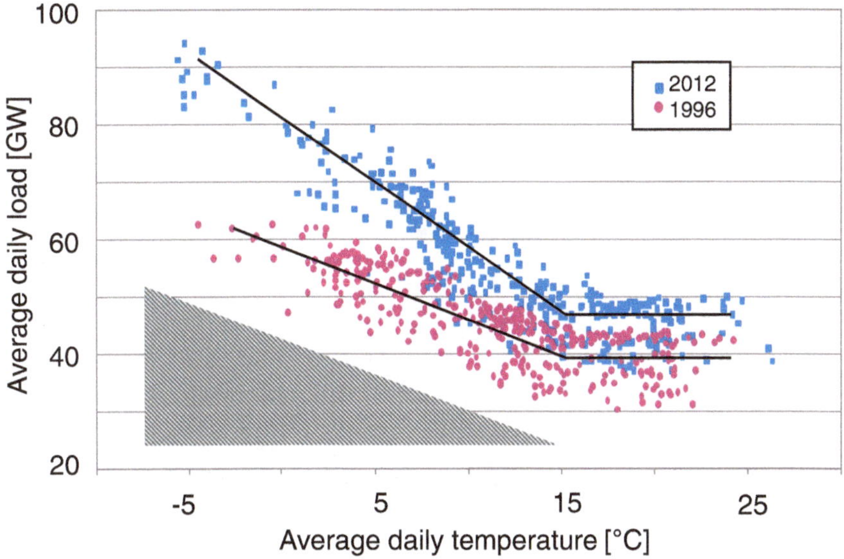

Figure 5: Determination and development of the heating gradient in 1996 and 2012 (adapted from RTE 2014).

Figure 6 shows the evolution of the French peak demand over the last decades. Especially in the time after 2000, the French peak load increased and became increasingly volatile, exceeding 100 GW in the winter 2011/12. This increase poses a serious threat to the French security of supply, and is mainly caused by the intransparency of electricity prices for end consumers. Through profiled consumers and unflexible tariffs, the scarcity in the system is disguised for the end consumers. RTE states, that an increase of price transparency, e.g. through flexible tariffs, may be able to significantly flexibilise the French electricity demand. This demand response potential in the residential sector shall be deployed in the next years, particularly fostered by the capacity mechanism. (RTE 2014)

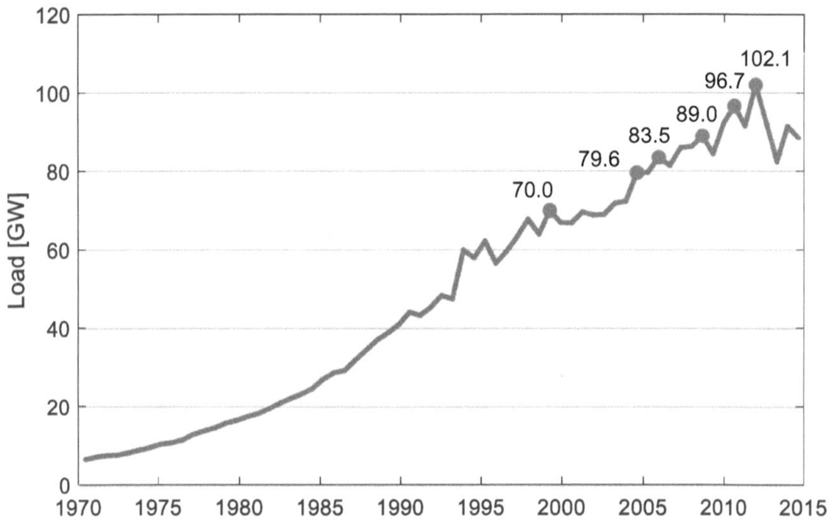

Figure 6: Evolution of the French peak load, effect of electrical heating (adapted from RTE 2014).

In terms of demand response measures, France used to have a total capacity of 6 GW in monopoly times, which were subsidised by EDF[1]. However, in the course of the market liberalisation, most of the interruptible load contracts expired and were not prolonged. As a result, in the current system

[1] Mainly decentralised emergency diesel generators in industrial sites were contracted to be activated in peak load periods to reduce the feed-out from the grid. Information obtained by RTE expert consultation.

there is around 3.5 GW of demand response capacity (RTE 2017b). A further deployment of demand response in future is likely, as the capacity mechanism seems to provide appropriate incentives to invest in peak load reduction measures.

2.3. France in the European Context

The French electricity system is part of the European Internal Market, thus in the majority of hours the French market is coupled with the neighbouring electricity markets. In scarcity hours in France, the neighbouring countries contribute with a significant share to the provision of security of supply and the reduction of the shortfall risk. However, this contribution is limited by the cross-border transfer capacities. See Table 1 for the net transfer capacities at the different borders that were available for import and export in the winter months of 2016.

Table 1: NTC values in winter months 2016 (RTE 2017c).

2016	January	February	March	November	December
[MW]	Import/ Export	Import/ Export	Import/ Export	Import/ Export	Import/ Export
Germany	2900/ 3500	3000/ 2300	1900/ 1700	1650/ 2500	4200/ 3250
England	2000/ 2000	2000/ 2000	2000/ 2000	2000/ 2000	1000/ 1000
Belgium	1150/ 3600	1200/ 3250	850/ 2850	700/ 1950	2000/ 2850
Spain	1750/ 2200	300/ 1400	300/ 1400	1300/ 2200	1300/ 2200
Italy	1160/ 2427	1160/ 2995	1160/ 373	1160/ 2427	1160/ 1494
Switzerland	2200/ 3200	1500/ 3200	1300/ 3200	1400/ 3200	1400/ 3200

It must be considered, that these transfer capacities are not necessarily available to the full extent and thus it is hazardous for the French electricity system to rely on the availability to be able to guarantee the security of supply. For example, in December 2016, January and February 2017 a transmission line connecting France and the UK was damaged and instead of 2000 MW only 1000 MW were available (Reuters 2016). Nevertheless, as load peaks in the European countries typically do not appear simultaneously, the abroad contribution is considered in the security of supply assessment. In the capacity mechanism, too, the foreign contribution is respected, as the capacity certificate obligation for the demand side does not match the peak demand, but is reduced by the security factor (see chapter 3.2).

2.4. Justification for a Capacity Remuneration Mechanism

As seen in the chapters above, the French electricity system is sensitive to extreme temperature events. The extreme situations in February 2012 and January 2017, where scarcity reached a critical level, showed the vulnerability of the French electricity system and prompted the French government to take action. As pointed out in 2.2, in the last years the French electricity system faces an increasing peak load as well as an increasing volatility of the peak load due to electrical heating. Thus it can be stated, that France has a peak load problem that endangers the security of supply and needs to be solved to prevent more critical scarcity situations in the future. However, the increasing share of renewables in the system exacerbates the uncertainty in the electricity system as the feed-in by renewables is fluctuating and hardly dispatchable. Defining the residual load as the load subtracted by the renewable feed-in, the residual load almost equals the total load in scarcity hours, meaning that renewable only slightly contribute to the security of supply.

The question that is addressed in this section is therefore, why the energy-only market is not able to guarantee the security of supply in the French market area and an additional remuneration scheme is necessary. Indeed, several analyses have attempted to answer this question in the past, identifying several issues leading to the lack of investments and to endangering the security of supply in energy-only markets. Among them risk aversion of investors, asymmetric investment incentives and flaws of the energy-only market are the most prominent (cf. e.g. Vázquez et al. 2002, Finon & Pignon 2008, Joskow 2008, Keppler 2017).

The issue of uncertainty of revenues and the resulting lack of investments due to risk aversion especially applies for peak generation plants. The profitability of investments in peak plants strongly depends on the occurrence and extent of price spikes. With the contribution margins in these few hours of spike prices, the plants need to cover their fix costs and investment payments in order to be profitable. However, especially if the spike prices depend on extreme weather events like in the French market area, they are associated with a high degree of uncertainty. As investors take decisions typically with uncertain information and in a risk averse manner, the energy-only market does not provide sufficient certain investment incentives (Finon & Pignon 2008). In the recent years, the expansion of renewable energies and the resulting merit order effect additionally lowers the profitability of power plants and makes their revenues more uncertain. The consequence is a lack of investments in peak power plants, leading to an insufficient security of supply level.

A second issue that is mentioned when analysing the reasons for a lack of peak capacity in systems with energy-only markets consists of the asymmetric investment incentives. De Vries and Heijnen (2008) mentioned the discrepancy between the social optimum and the theoretical outcome on the energy-only market (even under perfect knowledge) as a central conclusion of their investigation of investments under uncertainty and the effectiveness of capacity mechanisms. The theoretical reasoning for this asymmetry is thoroughly discussed by Keppler (2017). The inelastic demand curve in the electricity market leads to incentives for suppliers to underinvest. In this sense, the plant operators profit more from a slight scarcity than from an investment that leads to installed capacity exceeding the peak demand. Respecting that investment decisions are discrete, the argument for not investing in the marginal plant, but leaving a capacity gap is the following: The additional quantity sold by the additional unit does not lead to an overall profit increase for the supplier, because the overall revenue losses triggered by the price drop outweigh the revenue gains from the additional quantity sold. Thus, for each supply company it is better to not invest in the marginal generation unit, but to leave a capacity gap and profit from the higher prices caused by the scarcity.

In addition, market design flaws are adduced to explain the lack of investments in peak plants. Keppler (2017) points out why the benchmark model[2] cannot be assumed in the real-world market. In addition to the reasons mentioned above, the presence of an administrative price cap that is below the VoLL, leads to missing money for peak power plants and thus prevents sufficient investments to peak power plants. However, as Joskow (2008) observed, price caps are empirically rarely a binding constraint. This means that despite there are physical scarcity situations in the electricity system, the observed market prices do not reach the price cap, but remain on a lower level. In consequence, the theoretical missing money as the deviation between the VoLL and the price cap during scarcity hours is not the actual problem in reality, but the inability of the market to create sufficient price spikes. Reasons for the deviation between theoretical and empirical peak pricing are as well addressed in 4.2 of the present work.

The sections above summarised how the lack of sufficient investments in the energy-only market and the resulting threat to the security of supply is explained by economics theory. A solution in this context is the implementation of capacity remuneration mechanisms, which can be designed diversely. See e.g. RTE (2014, p. 44) for a classification of possible mechanism designs. With the capacity remuneration mechanism, the flaws of the energy-only market shall be counteracted and the provision of the public

2 The benchmark model states, that in competitive energy-only markets adequate and welfare-maximising capacity levels are reached due to VoLL pricing.

good security of supply shall be guaranteed in an effective and cost-efficient way (Poignant & Sido 2010).

The justification for the capacity mechanism is based on its ability to provide sufficient investment incentives to risk-averse investors and to resolve the flaws of the energy only market. On the one hand, a capacity remuneration mechanism translates the complex value of the public good security of supply and uncertainties related to price spikes into a capacity price with a corresponding risk, that is better manageable by investors (Keppler 2017). On the other hand, it provides incentives to demand responses measures that exceed the current level. An expansion of demand response capacities leads to a more flexi of the demand curve, which can counteract the asymmetry of investment incentives. As a consequence of the capacity remuneration mechanism complementing the energy-only market, the welfare-optimal electricity system that guarantees the security of supply shall evolve, containing both sufficient peak generation capacities and a more elastic demand. Capacity remuneration is thus considered the mean to solve the problem of missing peak load generation respectively the inelastic demand and the resulting threat to security of supply in scarcity situations.

However, in addition to the peak load problem, that is the urgent concern of the French government and at which decentralised capacity remuneration mechanism is addressed at, a mid and long term generation adequacy issue arises in the French market area as well. As seen in section 2.1, the base load provision strongly depends on the nuclear plant fleet. As shown by Zimmermann et al. (2017), in the 15 years between 2026 and 2041 almost 50 GW of nuclear capacity will exceed a lifetime of 50 years. New investments or substantial retrofit measures associated with large investment activities are thus inevitable in the mid and long term to sustain a functioning electricity system. Having analysed the rationale and intention of the introduced capacity remuneration mechanism, it is obvious, that the mechanism does not address base load issues, but is designed to solve the problem of missing peak load generation respectively missing demand adaption in scarcity hours. When the nuclear investment phase comes closer, caution must be paid to avoid the mechanism causing unnecessary costs. To incentivise investments in base load capacity either the energy-only market must prove its feasibility or different measures have to be implemented.

3. Decentralised Capacity Mechanism

3.1. A market-wide quantity-based Mechanism

As described in the previous section, the capacity mechanism shall provide sufficient incentives for investments to generation units or demand response measures. The market design suggested by RTE and chosen by the French government is a decentralised market-wide quantity-based capacity mechanism.

The quantity-based facet addresses the fact that no capacity price is fixed by authorities a priori, but the capacity price is determined via market procedure. This shall provide a cost-efficient way of providing the security of supply, as those technologies, which can provide the required capacity certificates in the cheapest way, are respected first. A market-based price formation provides incentives for both the demand side and the supply side to contribute to the provision of security of supply. Demand response measures deployed by the demand side can be marketed explicitly, i.e. on the market, or implicitly, i.e. lowering the capacity obligation and thus the demand for certificates.

The market-wide facet contains the design characteristic that on the supply side all generation capacities can participate, thus the mechanism does not focus on any specific technologies. On the demand side, all consumption is obliged to prove capacity certificates corresponding to their demand, including the grid operators in the amount of their system losses. The idea of the market-wide facet is to capture all consumers and their respective threat to the security of supply and let the consumers bear the appropriate costs for their contribution to the shortfall risk. On the supply side, all generation technologies shall be considered in the market-wide design, and be granted certificates in the amount their contribution to lowering the shortfall risk. As a consequence, the certification is based on the ability to generate during scarcity hours and the obligation is based on the consumption during scarcity hours. Like that, highly available generation units and consumption, that can be lowered in scarcity situations or does not contribute to the peak load extraordinarily strongly due to it is not temperature-sensitive, profit from the mechanism more than hardly dispatchable, unreliable generation units and very temperature sensitive consumption. (RTE 2014)

In comparison to a centralised capacity market, in which one central buyer acquires the certificates granted to the generation units, a decentralised capacity market involves the demand side much more. In the French mechanism design both the demand side, i.e. supply companies, large consumers and network operators, and the supply side, i.e. generation capacities and flexibilities, assess their certificate obligation respectively their certificate certification independently. Like that, the demand side is respected to be adaptive and demand-side reactions, which can lower the shortfall risk to the same amount as additional generation capacities, are triggered as well by the mechanism. Thus, a decentralised mechanism shall be more cost-efficient than a centralised mechanism. However, increased transaction costs need to be considered as well in the real-world implementation. See Figure 7 for the general logic of the French capacity mechanism.

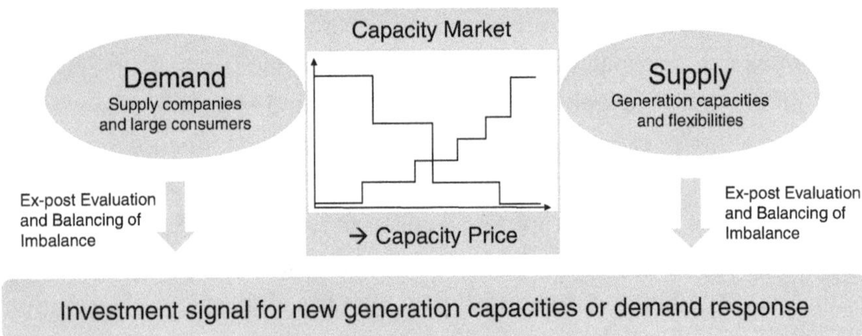

Figure 7: General logic of the decentralised capacity mechanism; adapted from RTE (2014), picture: EPEX Spot (2017).

The main objective of the capacity mechanism is to ensure the security of supply of France by meeting the reliability target of three hours of loss load, which is set by law. This objective shall be met by creating investment signals to investors on both the demand and the supply side to lower the shortfall risk. However, the mechanism shall not interfere with the electricity market but work as a complement to it addressing its inability to generate sufficient investment incentives. (RTE 2014)

In the following, the regulatory framework of the French capacity mechanism is presented in detail, followed by the analysis of the revision requested by the European Commission and the presentation of the first market results for the delivery year 2017.

3.2. Presentation of Regulatory Framework

This chapter provides a presentation of the regulatory framework elaborated by RTE and published by the French government in the context of the decree of 29 November 2016 (MEEM 2016). It consists of three separate units: First, the determination and evaluation of the capacity obligation for the obligated parties. Second, the determination and evaluation of the capacity certification for generators. Third, the market design and auction procedure, in which the certificates are traded. Note that currently the legislative text is only available in French.

The determination of the certificate obligation is done by each obligated party independently and at own responsibility. Since the mechanism is market-wide, all consumption and network system losses in the French market area are captured. The obligated parties thus contain supply companies supplying end consumers, self-supplying large consumers and network operators. Each obligated party determines its capacity obligation based on two factors: the expected consumption during scarcity situations and the security factor, which is calculated and published by RTE.

The security factor was implemented to parametrise the total demand for capacity certificates and shall ensure, that the security of supply target of three hours LOLE is neither exceeded nor undercut, but is exactly met. It particularly respects the contribution of electricity imports in scarcity situations to reduce the shortfall risk. To determine the value of the security factor, first the reference mix is determined and then divided by the reference power. The reference power is obtained by simulating the French electricity system in 100 weather scenarios, which are provided by Meteo France and consist of hourly intervals, and taking the 100 hours of largest consumption from each of the scenarios. The reference power then corresponds to the average load of these 10,000 hours of largest consumption under different weather conditions and amounts to 99.7 GW, being an estimate for the future peak load.

The reference mix corresponds to the amount of available capacity, i.e. certified capacity, that is required to meet the security of supply target, and is determined applying a supply-demand balance analysis for the considered delivery year. Over several demand scenarios the LOLE shall thus be exactly three hours in average. In the analyses conducted by RTE, the obtained reference mix amounted to 93 GW, thus the amount of certified capacity necessary to meet the security of supply target is 93 GW. As a consequence, the security factor as the ratio of reference mix and reference power for the first delivery years is set to 0.93 by RTE.

The security factor can be translated to the share of reliably available capacity in the peak load to ensure the security of supply is ensured. Having a security factor of 0.93 therefore means that the non-certified share of the installed generation capacities and the import of electricity from neighbouring countries reliably contribute to seven percent of the peak demand.

As a consequence the overall capacity obligation for obligated parties needs to be the expected peak demand in scarcity situations reduced by seven percent to avoid an excess demand. Such an excess demand would lead to inappropriately high prices and a security of supply level that exceeds the target, related to inappropriately high additional system costs. The obligated party thus only has to buy certificates in the amount of the security factor multiplied with its estimated demand during the peak period.

As the French load and hence demand of many obligated parties is strongly temperature-sensitive, RTE as well publishes a reference temperature for each delivery year. It consists of a time series of temperatures for a typical day of peak demand, in half-hourly resolution (see Table 2). The reference temperature provides the obligated parties a basis to estimate their demand and was fixed to the following time series for the years 2017 until 2020.

Table 2: Reference temperature values for 2017-2020 (RTE 2017d).

step	*Negative* temperature value in °C											
1-12	3.6	3.6	3.6	3.7	3.7	3.7	3.8	3.8	3.9	3.9	4.0	4.0
13-24	4.0	3.8	3.7	3.6	3.5	3.4	3.3	3.1	2.7	2.4	2.1	1.9
25-36	1.8	1.8	1.7	1.7	1.6	1.6	1.6	1.8	2	2.2	2.3	2.6
37-48	2.8	2.9	3.1	3.3	3.3	3.4	3.5	3.6	3.6	3.6	3.6	3.6

Based on their own pre-estimation, the obligated parties buy certificates on the capacity market. However, the self-responsible pre-estimations of all obligated parties are verified by RTE and checked whether the aggregated pre-estimations match the determined overall obligation level for the considered delivery period. If there is a significant deviation, RTE publishes the deviation.

After the delivery year, the capacity obligation is evaluated by RTE ex-post by analysing the periods of highest shortfall risk. For this purpose the peak period 1 (PP1) is defined. PP1 consists of 10 to 15 days per delivery year, which are selected from the delivery periods of a delivery year. A day is announced to be part of PP1 the day before, based on a demand forecast taking into account statistical distributions of historical load and the weather forecast. If a day is identified to be part of PP1, the 10 hours from 7am till 3pm and from 6pm till 8pm are added to PP1. Thus, the PP1 consists of 100 to 150 hours per delivery year.

The hours of the PP1 are used in the ex-post evaluation to determine the actual consumption during the period of highest shortfall risk and hence the capacity obligation of the obligated party. To relieve the obligated parties from the risk of extreme weather events, the measured consumption is corrected by the deviation of the temperature measured from the reference temperature fixed by RTE. The temperature gradient for each obligated party in a half-hour step is determined by running a linear regression over the half-hourly changes of demand on the respective half-hourly changes of temperature[3]. Like that, for each obligated party a temperature gradient for each half-hour step is determined. The general formula for the capacity obligation of an obligated party OP is as follows[4]:

$$Oblig_{OP,DY} = \frac{SF_{DY}}{2 * number\ of\ hours\ PP1(DY)} * \sum_{h \in PP1(DY)} \left[Cons_{OP,h} + P_{DR,OP,h} + TGrad_{OP,h} * (T_{ref,h,DY} - T_{act,h,DY})\right]$$

with the security factor in delivery year DY SF_{DY}, the half-hour steps h in PP1, the observed consumption of OP in the half-hour step h $Cons_{OP,h}$, the load of demand response measures activated by OP in step h $P_{DR,OP,h}$,

[3] The half-hour steps considered for the temperature gradient determination are taken from the days of the delivery year, excluding weekends and holidays.

[4] The ratio of the capacity obligation and the security factor is also referred to as the reference power of the obligated party.

the temperature gradient of OP in step h $TGrad_{OP,h}$, the reference temperature in step h of delivery year DY $T_{ref,h,DY}$ and the actual temperature in step h $T_{act,h,DY}$.

Note, that the consumption can consist, depending on the obligated party, of a remotely metered part, a profiled part and a losses part. Going more into detail on how the consumption time series is obtained would exceed the scope of this work, but can be found in the legislative text.

As can be seen in the formula, high attention is paid on the correct consideration of the temperature sensitivity of each obligated party. This respects the aspiration of the capacity mechanism to let the consumers pay for the security of supply appropriately to their contribution to the shortfall risk. Thus, parties that are able to reduce their load in peak periods and are less temperature-sensitive face a lower capacity obligation than parties with a strong temperature sensitivity and an inflexible consumption.

The certification of capacity entities on the supply side is as well performed in a decentralised manner. The term capacity entity hereby contains actual generation units as well as sheddable loads, as their activation has the same impact on avoiding a situation of critical scarcity or even a shortfall. Both existing capacities and capacities on project stage, that will be operational in the delivery year, can be certified. For capacity entities upper and lower limits of certification are provided by the regulatory framework. Within these limits, an owner can certify his capacity entity according to the realisation-based approach described in the following sections.

The certification limits are defined by the reference value, the acceptability margin and the installed capacity. The reference value is calculated as the installed capacity multiplied with a technology-specific capacity credit. See the following table for the capacity credits of the most common technologies.

Table 3: Capacity credits for relevant technologies (RTE 2017d).

Technology	*Capacity Credit*
Nuclear	90%
Coal	88%
Gas	88%
Hydro pumped storage/ run-of-river	80% / 50%
Wind onshore / offshore	20% / 25%
Photovoltaic	5%
Biomass	80%

The acceptability margin is a well given as a technology-specific percentage and determines the degree to which the certification can deviate from the reference value as a percentage of the installed capacity. Value for the most common technologies are provided in the following table.

Table 4: Acceptability margins for relevant technologies (RTE 2017d).

Technology	*Acceptability margin*
Nuclear	7%
Coal	10%
Gas	10%
Hydro pumped storage	7%
Hydro run-of-river	25%

Wind onshore	7%
Wind offshore	7%
Photovoltaic	5%
Biomass	10%

The resulting certification range is calculated using the following formula:

$$range^{Certification} = [P^{ref}_{entity} - (P^{inst}_{entity} * m^{accept}_{technology}); P^{ref}_{entity} + (P^{inst}_{entity} * m^{accept}_{technology})],$$

with the reference value of the capacity entity P^{ref}_{entity}, the installed capacity P^{inst}_{entity} and the acceptability margin for the used technology $m^{accept}_{technology}$.

For better understanding, an example shall be provided. Hence, consider a nuclear power plant with an installed capacity of 1000 MW, the technology-specific capacity credit of 90 percent and the technology-specific acceptability margin of 7 percent. The reference value for the nuclear power plant would be 900 MW and the applying the formula the resulting certification range results in [830 MW; 970 MW]. Thus, the owner of the plant can determine the amount of certificates granted between 830 MW and 970 MW.

The exact certification of the capacity entity is done by the fixation of the parameters available power, infra-daily availability factor K_h, intra-daily availability factor K_j and the technology-specific controllability factor $C_{technology}$. These need to be fixed in the certification request the capacity operator gives to RTE, but however contain a certain degree of freedom.

The available power equals the best available estimate of the power that will be available in the PP2[5] of the considered delivery year and is thus a very vague term. The infra-daily availability factor K_h is defined by the number of PP2 hours, in which the capacity can be activated on a PP2 day. The number of activation hours can be determined by the capacity operator and is in the range of 0 to 10, which translates to the factor K_h following the table below.

Table 5: Values of the infra-daily availability factor Kh (RTE 2017d).

Number of hours	0.5	1	1.5	2	2.5
K_h	13%	25%	35%	46%	53%
Number of hours	3	3.5	4	4.5	5
K_h	59%	65%	70%	74%	78%
Number of hours	5.5	6	6.5	7	7.5
K_h	82%	85%	88%	91%	93%
Number of hours	8	8.5	9	9.5	10
K_h	95%	96%	98%	99%	100%

[5] PP2 stands for peak period 2 and can be compared to the PP1 used for the ex-post evaluation of the capacity obligation. The PP2 contains the 10 to 25 days of highest load of a delivery year and is used to evaluate the capacity certification ex-post. By definition, each PP1 day is as well a PP2 day. In addition, up to ten more days can be announced as PP2 day by RTE the day before, based on the demand forecast. Analog to the PP1, for each PP2 day only the hours from 7am till 3pm and from 6pm till 8pm are considered, thus resulting in a PP2 containing 100 to 250 hours.

The intra-daily availability factor K_j is defined by the number of consecutive days the capacity can be activated within a week containing five consecutive PP2 days and thus ranges between 0 and 5. The number of activation days translates to the factor K_j according to the table below.

Table 6: Values of the intra-daily availability factor Kj (RTE 2017d).

Number of consecutive days	0	1	2	3	4	5
K_j	0%	45%	73%	88%	94%	100%

The controllability factor $C_{technology}$ respects the extent to which the generation of a technology can be controlled. It thus is different from 100 percent only for hardly dispatchable capacities. For all thermal capacities it is set to 100 percent, the values for the relevant technologies are provided in the table below

Table 7: Controllability factors for relevant technologies (RTE 2017d).

Technology	*Controllability factor*
Hydro run-of-river	85%
Wind onshore	70%
Wind offshore	70%
Photovoltaic	25%
All other energy technologies	100%

As can be derived from the presentation of the certification parameters, the capacity owner has a certain degree of freedom in the certification of his capacity. Only the certification range works as an actual constraint as the certified capacity level has to be within the fixed range. The formula for the calculation of the certified capacity level (NCC, niveau de capacité certifié) using the parameters is as follows:

$$NCC_{entity} = P_{entity}^{avail} * K_{h,entity} * K_{j,entity} * C_{technology}$$

with the available power of the capacity entity P_{entity}^{avail}, the infra-daily availability factor $K_{h,entity}$, the intra-daily availability factor $K_{j,entity}$ and the technology-specific controllability factor $C_{technology}$.

However, for renewable capacities that are subject to meteorological conditions, an alternative approach (called régime dérogatoire) to determine the certified capacity is feasible. The owner can hereby choose between the realisation-based certification approach presented in the sections above and a normative approach. The normative approach[6] is based on historical feed-in patterns of the installation or on representative feed-in patterns, if the installation has no sufficient historical data. Historical feed-in patterns can be applied for wind and solar, if five consecutive years of historical feed-in data are available for the installation. For run-of-river installations, ten years of historical data are required.

The certified capacity level (NCC) for a renewable capacity certified via the normative approach is calculated as follows:

[6] In the draft rules published in 2014 (RTE 2014), the normative approach consisted of multiplying the installed capacity with a technology-specific capacity credit. This simplified methodology was changed in the final rules, to respect regional diversification of the renewable's availability. Thus, wind capacities close to the shore can expect a higher certification than those more inland and solar capacities in the south can expect a higher certification than those in the north.

$$NCC_{entity} = C_{technology} * \frac{\sum_{i=1}^{N} \sum_{h \in PP2(DY-i-4)} P_h^{feed-in}}{number\ of\ hours\ \in PP2\ of\ considered\ years}$$

with the technology-specific controllability factor $C_{technology}$, the number of considered years N, the historical feed-in in hour h taken from the historical data or a representative feed-in pattern of $P_h^{feed-in}$ and the PP2 period of a past year i $PP2(i)$. The formula can be paraphrased casually as the average historical feed-in in the considered PP2 periods multiplied with the controllability factor.

In the sections above, the determination of the obligation and the level of certification was presented. As the mechanism parameters reference temperature and security factor are published by RTE for years prior to the delivery year (DY-4), the certification level and obligation for the market participants can be determined four years prior to the delivery year, too. RTE also publishes the overall obligation level, which equals the reference power described before. However, for the certification deadlines, existing capacities, capacities at project stage and demand response capacities are distinguished. Existing capacities have to hand in their certification request in DY-4 the latest two months before DY-3 starts, thus until 1 November DY-4. Capacities at project stage need to request the certification two months before the considered delivery year the latest (until 1 November DY-1) or if appropriate two months after the initial commissioning. Demand response capacities need to request the certification in the period DY-4 until two months before the considered delivery years starts, i.e. until 1 November DY-1.

Within the period DY-4 and DY-1, the actual capacity auctions take place. Once the market is mature, for each delivery year at least 15 auctions shall take place according to the schedule: one in DY-4, four in DY-3, four in DY-2 and six auctions in DY-1. In the auctions the obligated parties can buy their required certificates and capacity owners can sell their capacity certificates. The auctions are organised by EPEX Spot and the auction results as well as the bidding curves are published. Each auction is a single-price auction and has an administrative price cap. During the transition years, the price caps are 20,000 € per MW for delivery year 2017, 40,000 € per MW for the delivery years 2018 and 2019 and 60,000 € per MW for delivery year 2020. From 2021 on, the CONE shall serve as the administrative price cap. Next to the capacity auctions, over-the-counter (OTC) trading is possible as well via bilateral contracts between obligated parties and certificate owners.

The calendrical structure of the mechanism is provided in Figure 8. Note that the dates after the delivery years have been changed compared to the draft rules published in 2014 and are now at a later point of time.

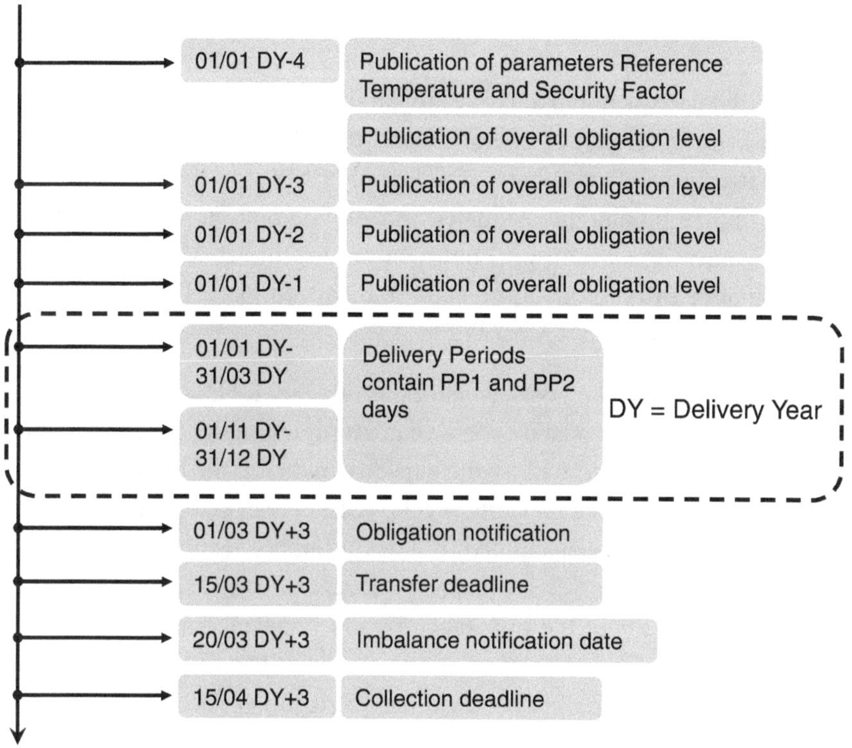

Figure 8: Calendrical structure of the capacity mechanism (own illustration based on RTE 2014), adapted to dates provided by (MEEM 2016).

The delivery year consists of two delivery periods, containing the period 1 January until 31 March and 1 November until 31 December. Within the delivery periods of a delivery year, RTE can announce a day to be a PP1 respectively a PP2 day on the day before. The ex-post evaluation of the capacity obligations is conducted by RTE based on the PP1 days, whereas the ex-post evaluation of the certification levels is conducted based on the PP2 days.

For the obligated parties, the ex-post evaluation is based on the data of the PP1 hours transmitted by the respective grid operator to RTE. RTE then calculates the actual capacity obligation with the realisations of consumption and temperature according to the formula described before. Note, that the obligated party is not taken to responsibility, if the realised temperature was below the reference temperature and thus does not have to bear the risk of extreme weather events. If a deviation between the pre-estimated capacity obligation and the evaluated capacity obligation is identified, the obligated party is notified until notification deadline 1 March of DY+3. The imbalance of the portfolio has to be balanced via OTC trading until the collection deadline 15 April DY+3.

For capacity entities, the post-evaluation is done by RTE according to data of the PP2 hours of the past delivery year. Applying these, the certification parameter values transmitted by the capacity owner in the certification are verified and the effective capacity level (NCE, niveau de capacité effectif) of the capacity entity is calculated. If a deviation between the certified capacity level and the effective capacity level is identified, the capacity owner is notified about the imbalance by the imbalance notification date 20 March DY+3. The imbalance of the portfolio has to be balanced via OTC trading until the collection deadline 15 April DY+3.

For renewable energies, that were certified using the normative approach, a different evaluation methodology is applied. As the fluctuating and hardly dispatchable character of the installations was already considered in the certification process, the availability is only evaluated in the sphere of the owner's influence. In this sense, it is checked in how many hours of the PP2 hours the installation was in technical state to generate electricity, complying an effective availability rate. Consequently, the capacity owner is not responsible for unfavourable weather conditions and thus is not exposed to the weather risk. If the capacity was operational in PP2 all hours of the delivery year, the effective capacity level equals the certified capacity level, even if the historical feed-in pattern was not realised in the considered delivery year. Whereas, if the installation had a technical outage during the PP2, the effective capacity level is reduced appropriately and the capacity owner has an imbalance.

However, it has to be stated that the late notification dates and collection deadline are due to a thorough ex-post evaluation by RTE. If the market participant identifies a deviation by himself, OTC trading to balance the portfolio can be performed in the entire period until the collection deadline. Thus, it is likely that market participants already evaluate their performance during the PP1 and PP2 to estimate their imbalance and to react timely.

If the imbalance of a market participant is not balanced after the collection deadline, a penalty scheme applies. For this purpose, a market reference price is determined by the regulation authority CRE (Commission de Régulation de l'Énergie). The exact methodology, with which de market reference price is determined is not fixed yet. For the first delivery year however it was set to the clearing price of the capacity auction for the delivery year. In the law that is currently in state, the determination of the reference price is not addressed. For the revision expected to be in state from 2019 on, the definition of a methodology is planned. To calculate the penalty for imbalance, the unitary price, which has to be paid for the imbalance, of delivery year DY $P_{DY}^{unitary}$ is defined as follows:

$$P_{DY}^{unitary} = \begin{cases} (1-k) * P_{DY}^{ref}, & if\ imb > 0, \\ (1+k) * P_{DY}^{ref}, & if\ -1\,GW < imb < 0, \\ \left(2 - \frac{(1-k)}{|imb|}\right) * P_{DY}^{ref}, & if\ imb < -1\,GW, \end{cases}$$

with the market reference price of delivery year DY P_{DY}^{ref}, the imbalance volume imb and the penalty coefficient k. The penalty coefficient k determines, to which extent an imbalance lower than 1 GW is penalised, and is currently defined to 0.2. If the imbalance exceeds the threshold of 1 GW, for the remaining imbalance, twice the market reference price must be paid.

See Figure 9 for an illustration, compared to the imbalance settlement only using the market reference price.

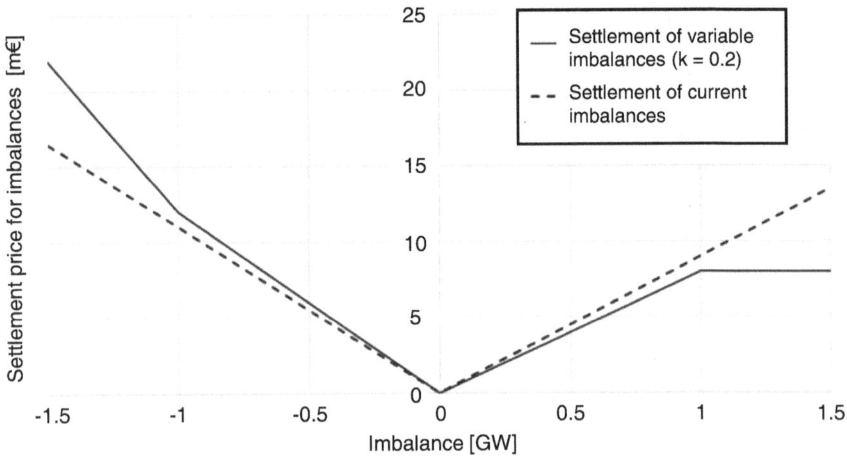

Figure 9: Payments for imbalance settlements, assuming a market reference price of 10,000 € per MW; adapted from EC (2016).

As seen in chapter 2.1, the French market area is strongly dominated by EDF, as the former monopolist still operates the nuclear power plants. To avoid a distortion of the capacity mechanism by market power and prevent EDF from applying strategic behaviour, some design facets where introduced against the abuse of market power. However, the European Commission treats several issues in their decision of 8 November 2016 (EC 2016). The measures described in the following are already part of the in-state law, further revisions requested by the European Commission are discussed in chapter 3.3.

The measures against market power address a possible strategic offering of certificates in the auctions and the withhold of capacity certificates. The concern is, that EDF is able to influence the liquidity as well as the clearing price of capacity auctions essentially and thus can offer its certificates strategically. As a consequence, a withholding of capacity certificates would result in high capacity certificate prices and possibly a high market reference price. As there is a shortage of certificates in the capacity auctions, the obligated parties are forced to buy certificates at a higher price on the OTC market to fulfil their capacity obligation.

To mitigate such a market power abuse, every capacity supplier has to respect to certification range mentioned above to not underestimate his certified capacity. Each supplier with more than 3 GW certified capacity is obliged to offer the certified capacities according to a quantity schedule. This measure shall guarantee market liquidity and avoid distortion through withholding of capacity certificates. However, the threshold of 3 GW only applies for EDF. The schedule is as follows: 25 percent of certified capacity certificates must be offered in the auctions in DY-4. In the auctions of DY-3, the maximum out of 25 percent of certified capacity certificates and 25 percent of the certificates that have not been previously sold has to be offered. In the auctions of DY-2, the maximum out of 25 percent of certified capacity certificates and 50 percent of the certificates that have not been previously sold has to be offered. Finally, In the auctions of DY-1, the maximum out of 25 percent of certified capacity certificates and 100 percent of the certificates that have not been previously sold has to be offered.

This schedule shall guarantee liquidity in the capacity auctions and avoid a strategic withholding of certificates to sell them at a later stage at a scarcity price or profiting from an increased market reference price. In addition, the market reference price is not determined by the capacity auction clearing prices, but by the independent authority CRE.

Apart from all mentioned measures, the Cartel Authority (Autorité de la Concurrence) observes the market procedures and participants' behaviours and reports if there a signs for a distorted competition.

3.3. Revisions requested by European Commission

As the French capacity mechanism cannot only be considered in the isolated French national context, but as well as an intervention of the French state in the European internal energy market, the European Commission conducted a sector inquiry to assess the conformity of the capacity mechanism proposed by RTE with the Internal Market. As a result, the European Commission classifies the capacity market as a state aid compatible to the Internal Market and authorises the capacity mechanism for a duration of ten years. (EC 2016)

However, the Commission requests some modifications in the mechanism design to ensure the conformity with European law, in particular to ensure the functioning of the liberalised energy market in France. These modifications shall be implemented in the revision of the capacity mechanism rules that are currently developed and will be in state from 2019 on.

The modification requests can be classified into three categories: securing the opportunity for cross-border participation, preventing the abuse of market power and creating investment certainty for new investments.

The opportunity for foreign capacity entities to participate in the French capacity mechanism is one of the core requests, as excluding foreign capacities from the capacity mechanism is an intervention in the functioning of the European Internal Market. Thus, the Commission demands, that foreign capacities must be allowed to participate in the mechanism, according to the physical constraints. However, the request may be just pro forma as in scarcity hours the neighbouring countries are already incentivised by price signals to export electricity in the amount of the cross-border transfer capacities. As these transfer capacities are auctioned by today, they are already economically exploited.

However, to follow the request the French government proposed an hybrid model, in which a foreign capacity owner must prove both his capacity certificates according to the certification rules and a transmission capacity ticket, which guarantees that the transfer capacity is secured for contributing to the reduction of the French shortfall risk. Like that, foreign capacities are allowed to participate in the French capacity mechanism and the request is met. It remains to be seen, if the participation in the capacity market will evolve as the most economic option for the use the cross-border transfer capacities or if the cross-border participation fails in the transfer capacity constraint. At least, the functioning of the Internal Market is not a priori distorted by generally excluding foreign capacities.

The second category addresses the prevention of the abuse of market power. Thus, two requests have to be met by the revision of the mechanism rules. First, a loophole allowing companies to transfer capacity certificates internally at zero costs shall be closed. For this purpose, company-internal trades must be carried out with prices that are representative for the market prices. The underlying concern of the Commission was, that otherwise the retail division of EDF or other companies with both generation and retail activity would have a significant market advantage over concurring retail companies without generation. To let all retail companies face the same economic conditions, internal trades thus have to be published and carried out on market price level. However, demand response deployment activities financed by the generation division of a company to lower the capacity obligation for the retail division are not captured by the modification and may as well represent an unequal competition.

The second request against the abuse of market power consist of the publication of all OTC trades in an anonymised manner. Hereby the date, the volume and the agreed price are published for each OTC trade. The publication shall guarantee the visibility of prices outside the capacity auctions and provide the required transparency to avoid collusion and uncompetitive price agreements between dominant companies. Conclusively, the Commission aims to strengthen the official capacity auctions by regulating OTC trade within business divisions of one company and the OTC trade within different companies. A side-effect of the requests might be as well an increase of the liquidity of the capacity auctions, as OTC trading becomes less attractive for some players.

The third category of modification requests addresses the investment in new capacity entities. In the current rules no specific design detail provides investment security to new investments. Newly built capacities are considered existing capacities from their first delivery year on and are thus exposed to market risks to the full extent. Since the capacity mechanism is not supposed to be only a remuneration scheme for existing capacities but shall provide incentives to foster new investments, the Commission requests an appropriate consideration of the risk aversion of investors. Thus, investment certainty shall be provided to new investments by means of an initial contract lasting the first seven delivery years. The contract is designed as a Contract for Difference, thus in the first seven years, the new capacity is paid the maximum out of an initial reference price fixed in the contract and the market reference price of the considered future delivery year. The determination of the initial reference price is not defined exactly yet, but will be similar to a weighted average taking into account the clearing prices of the auctions in DY-4 for the delivery years DY-1 and DY-2 as well as the clearing price for the auction for delivery year DY, thus aiming to be a representative and non-distorted price. See Figure 10 for a graphic illustration of which auctions are considered to determine the initial reference price.

The difference between contract price and the capacity auction clearing price in the years covered by the contract will be borne by the obligated parties[7]. Thus, the additional costs to provide investment security to new investments will most probably be over-rolled and paid by the end consumers.

[7] Information provided by RTE market analyst.

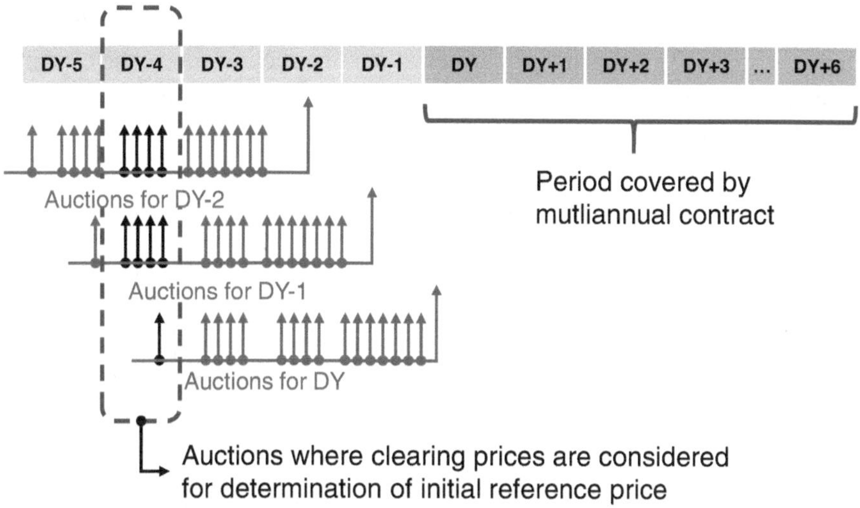

Figure 10: Determination of initial reference price for new investments (own illustration based on EC 2016).

The revised legislation shall be in state from 2019 on and be valid as of the beginning of the auctions for delivery year 2023. For the delivery years 2020, 2021 and 2022, a transitory legislation with multiannual contracts shall be defined to not impede new investments. In the transitory phase. However, the legislative text is still elaborated.

3.4. First Market Results

As 2017 is the first delivery year of the capacity mechanism, there has already been a capacity auction. It took place on 5 December 2016. In total, a volume of 22,358 MW was traded at a clearing price of 9,999.8 €/MW. Note, that the volume of one capacity certificate is 0.1 MW, thus the price per certificate is 999.98 € and the volume is 226,358 certificates. The bids on the demand side and on the supply side were published by EPEX Spot. See Figure 11 for an illustration of the demand and supply curves.

As expected, the supply curve is step-shaped and relatively price-elastic. This complies perfectly with the diversity of generation technologies, that are granted certificates, and their respective difference costs. The demand curve is relatively steep and price-inelastic in the section where the clearing took place. However, it can be observed that many ask bids anticipated the clearing price of roughly 10,000 € per MW, which results in the horizontal line at 10,000 €.

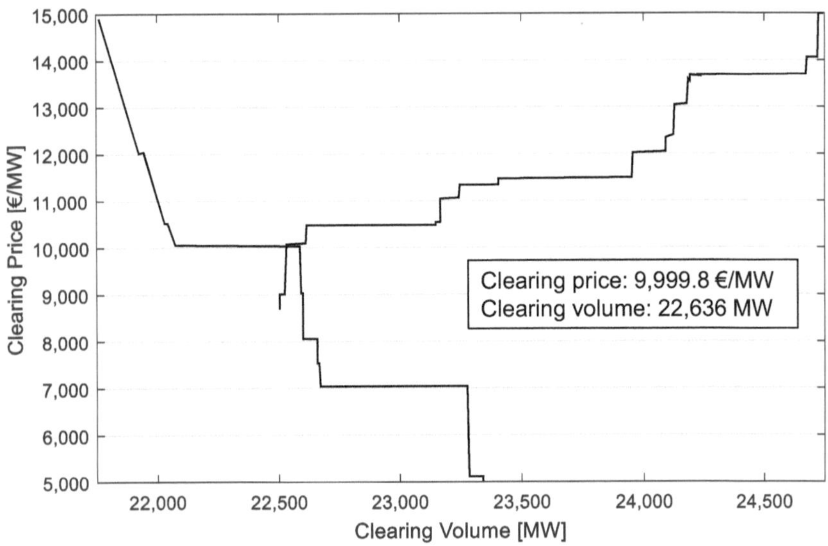

Figure 11: Demand and supply curve of first capacity auction of 15 December 2016 (own illustration based on EPEX Spot 2016).

In April 2017, the second capacity auction took place. The market clearing price was 10,419.4 € per MW, the traded volume was however only 516.7 MW. Further auctions and results remain to be seen.

4. Modelling a Decentralised Capacity Market

To analyse interactions and interdependencies of different mechanism parameters and to investigate the influence of the capacity mechanism on investment decisions and thus the future power plant park of France, the main part of the present work consists of modelling and implementing the French capacity mechanism. For this purpose, the existing agent-based power markets simulation model PowerACE was extended.

In the following sections the modelling approach is described in detail. It is structured as follows: Firstly, the simulation model PowerACE in general and its applications related to capacity mechanisms throughout the years are presented briefly. Following, the justification and need for an extension containing the French capacity mechanism is discussed. After the system boundaries and input data are stated, being the main part of this chapter the logic and methodology of the model are described in detail. In the end, alternative approaches that are used to model and analyse the French capacity mechanism are presented.

4.1. Presentation of Agent-based Simulation Model PowerACE

The agent-based power market simulation model PowerACE (cf. e.g. Genoese (2010), Keles et al. (2016a) or Ringler (2016) for a more detailed description) was developed at the Institute for Industrial Production (IIP) at the Karlsruhe Institute of Technology to simulate power markets in order to investigate investment decisions in a liberalised market environment. Figure 12 shows an overview over the model's logical structure. PowerACE contains computational agents for the different players involved in the market, such as plant operators or market operators, and depicts their respective behaviour. The main central market places are modelled, in particular the electricity spot market. Each player is hereby represented by several agents that fulfil functions and roles within the market logic, like e.g. trading on the spot market and investment planning.

The three core elements of PowerACE are the demand side, the supply side and the markets. In addition, the transmission system operator agent manages and markets the feed-in of renewable energies and a regulator agent gives the regulatory framework.

The electricity demand is exogenously loaded from the data base and consists of the future demand for the simulation period in hourly resolution. Taking into account the expected renewable feed-in and exchanges with neighbouring market areas, the residual demand, which needs to be covered by power plants offering electricity on the spot market, is determined. In this way, both the residual demand profile throughout the year and the long-term evolution of the residual peak demand is considered. Apart from demand response measures activated in hours of scarcity, PowerACE considers the demand to be price-inelastic on the spot market.

The supply side consists of the main supply companies, in the French case EDF, E.ON France, Poweo and GDF Suez as well as one agent operating the power plants which are not operated by any of the main supply companies. For these supply companies, PowerACE simulates both the short-term power plant dispatch and the long-term investment planning. Using data from the World Electric Power Plants (WEPP) database provided by Platts (Platts 2017), the existing power plants for each of the supply companies are captured by single generation unit. The techno-economic parameters provided for each unit are among others, installed capacity, energy carrier and technology, year of commissioning, efficiency, availability and emission factors. Considering these as well as exogenously given fuel and carbon prices, the supply trader determines the variable production costs of each unit and offers electricity on the day-ahead market. The offers are aggregated to obtain the supply curve. The residual demand and supply curve match determines electricity spot prices and the cost-optimal power plant dispatch for each supply company.

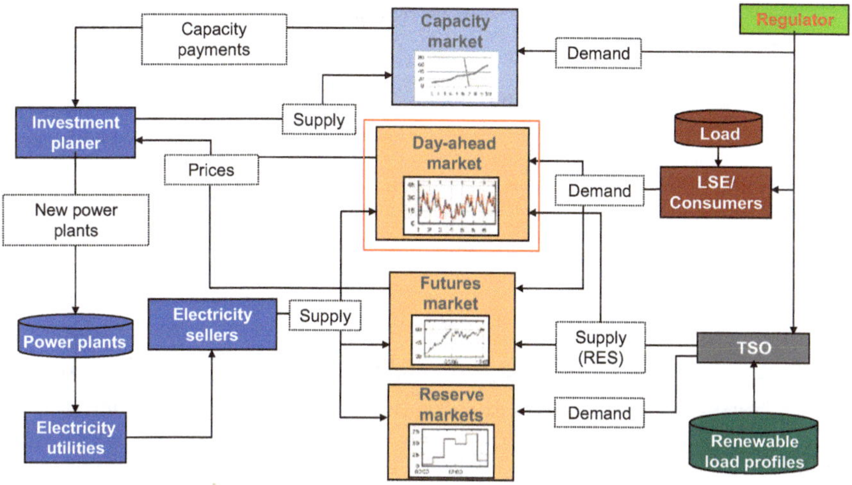

Figure 12: Schematic illustration of PowerACE structure (Keles et al. 2016a).

At the end of each simulation year, the supply companies take decommissioning and investment decisions. If a power plant was unprofitable for several consecutive year or reaches its technical lifetime, it is decommissioned. For the investment decision, each supply company has a computational agent for investment planning. Each investment planner has several investment options at its disposal, i.e. power plant options for different available technologies, and a long-term electricity price forecast. The investment options are assessed using the net present value approach, which takes into account the investment, the fixed costs and the expected cash flow generated on the electricity market. If there are additional incomes, e.g. generated through a capacity remuneration mechanism, they are considered in the investment appraisal as well. If an investment option has a positive net present value, a new power plant is built and added to the supplier's portfolio in the database. With this methodology, PowerACE determines the long-term development of the power plant park for a simulation horizon of up to 2050.

In its initial version, PowerACE consisted solely of the German market area and had no capacity mechanism. Over the years, many studies with various objectives have been conducted at the Institute for Industrial Production using the PowerACE model (see Ringler (2016, 95ff.) for an overview). Thus, there are a variety of PowerACE model extensions and advancements focusing on different research topics. One of these research topics addresses the question whether the investment incentives of energy-only markets are sufficient to guarantee the long-term generation adequacy or if additional revenues through capacity remuneration mechanisms are necessary to incentivize sufficient investments. Several capacity remuneration mechanism designs have been analysed with the PowerACE model for the German market area: Genoese et al. (2012) analysed a mechanism based on capacity payments, Renz et al. (2014) analysed a centralised capacity market design, Bublitz et al. (2015) analysed a strategic reserve, Keles et al. (2016b) analysed a strategic reserve as well as a decentralised and a centralised capacity market. More recently, Zimmermann et al. (2017) analysed the influence of the implementation of a decentralised capacity mechanism in the French market area. However, the mechanism design that was used for the latter is based on the VKU proposal design used in Keles et al. (2016b) and thus does not capture the properties of the French mechanism design sufficiently. For this reason, in the present work, the decentralised French capacity mechanism is modelled thoroughly according to the rules provided by RTE (MEEM 2016). This is done to analyse the mechanism and to assess the impacts it has on the long-term power plant park and generation adequacy evolution.

As can be derived from the number and variety of applications and advancements over the past years, PowerACE serves as a mature and reliable model environment and simulation resource which can be adapted to numerous applications. It thus serves as the basis for the model of the French capacity mechanism which is developed in the scope of the present work. In subchapter 4.3, the system boundaries and input data for the capacity mechanism model are described, followed by subchapter 0, in which the capacity mechanism model is described thoroughly. Section 4.2 treats the question of why a capacity mechanism is required in a simulation model such as PowerACE.

4.2. Necessity of a Capacity Mechanism in PowerACE

The agent-based simulation model PowerACE has been the base for several studies related to the electricity markets in Europe. Since its first deployment it has been further developed and improved by many studies with different objectives and market areas under consideration. The main objective in the majority of the studies was to analyse the development of the power plant park and the future evolution of electricity prices, under different framework conditions and scenarios (cf. e.g. Ringler et al. (2014) and Zimmermann et al. (2016)). But apart from the studies mentioned in subchapter 4.1, none of the studies considered a capacity remuneration mechanism to be necessary for the functioning of the energy only market and for securing the long-term generation adequacy. Thus, the question that has to be answered in this section is why a capacity remuneration mechanism should be necessary to be implemented in PowerACE and which benefits can be expected from adding a model extension, that simulates the French capacity market.

This subchapter does not address the question, if capacity mechanisms are in general necessary to from a theoretic perspective, but addresses the necessity of a capacity mechanism in the PowerACE model. The theoretical justification for a capacity mechanism in the French market area is discussed in chapter 2.4.

Indeed, PowerACE has been used in the past to prove the functioning of energy only markets and their ability incentivise sufficient investments to ensure the long-term generation adequacy. However, the outcome of a simulation is always determined substantially by the premises, by the input data and by assumptions. During the work with the PowerACE model in the scope of this work, one of the central insights was the huge impact of the long-term electricity price forecast on new investment activity. Thus, the approach and underlying assumptions used in the price forecast have a major impact on the development of the power plant park. In the base version of PowerACE, the forecast of electricity prices consists of matching the expected load with the expected available capacities. If there is a scarcity situation, demand response is considered. However, if the demand response measures cannot satisfy the demand either, a lack of generation capacity is identified and the forecasted price for the considered hour is the administrative price cap, i.e. 3000 € per MWh. This approach leads to forecasts containing many hours with the price cap, signalling the future scarcity and providing strong investment incentives for the supply companies. In this sense, PowerACE is modelling a non-distorted functioning of the markets, in which sufficient incentives are provided to investors to guarantee the long-term generation adequacy.

However, at this point PowerACE tends to suffer from the abstraction and is not depicting the real-world spot market prices, but overestimates the occurrence of hours with price cap in the forecast and thus too the expected profits for new investments on the electricity markets. The scarcity situations in the French market area caused by cold waves in February 2012 and January 2017 have shown that in the real world, the energy only market might not always be able to generate adequate price signals in scarcity situations to foster the necessary investments.

Whereas the cold temperatures led to a scarcity situation in the electricity system, the prices on the spot market did not reach the price cap in even a single hour but stayed below 2000 € per MWh, as Figure 1 displaying the hourly electricity prices in the week with the most scarce situation in

France from February 2012 shows (RTE 2012).

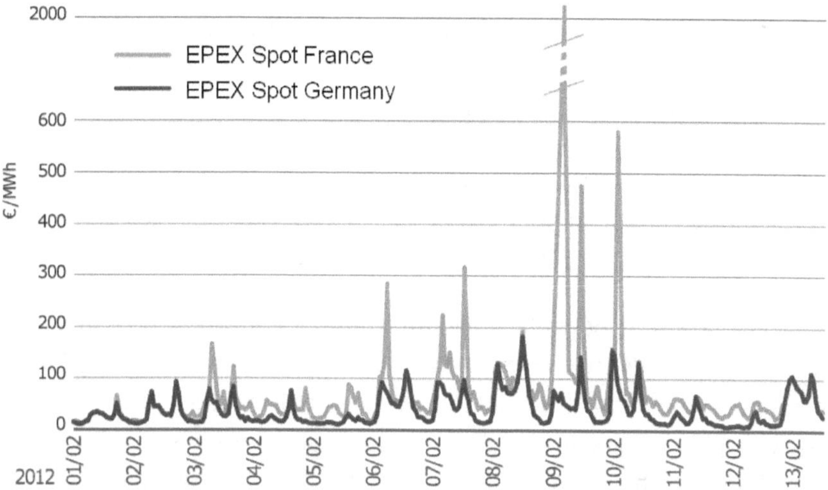

Figure 13: Spot prices of France and Germany in the period of the cold wave 1 till 13 February 2012. (RTE 2012)

The reasons for this deviation between scarcity prices expected in theory and empiric scarcity prices can be diverse. On the one hand, electricity exchange can lower the residual load, that needs to be covered by the French generation capacities. This is however already respected in PowerACE as exchange between market areas is modelled. On the other hand, demand response measures going beyond the level captured by the PowerACE model can lower the residual load, too.

Another possible option, which is rarely mentioned in scientific publications, is the deployment of shortfall mitigation measures in a scarcity situation, as mentioned by the Office for Gas and Electricity Markets of the UK Government. Where the economic theory and the current PowerACE forecast approach draw a sharp line between an adequate supply situation and a shortfall situation, in the physical electricity system, there is still a buffer for the system operators to mitigate an actual shortfall or a loss of load. These measures contain voltage control, maximum generation of capacities and emergency services on interconnectors and amount to roughly 2 GW for the UK electricity system (Ofgem 2014, p. 24). Indeed, these measures should be taken only after the market procedure and the reaching of the price cap to avoid a distortion of the energy-only market, as anticipation by market players would lower the resilience of the system and lead to lowering the security of supply (Ofgem 2014). However, these mitigation measures might be involved in the deviation between theoretical scarcity prices and the empiric scarcity prices, too.

In the end, even if not explained entirely, the deviation between theory and empiricism needs to be respected in a power markets model like PowerACE that aims to model the real market behaviour. It is unlikely to expect supply companies to take investment decisions based on theoretical price forecasts that exceed the price levels of empiric market results. For this purpose, the long-term price forecast approach needs to be modified slightly. As the risk of being scientifically inaccurate outweighs the benefit of having price forecasts that resemble empirical market prices exactly, the methodology is not changed substantially. The forecast logic and administrative price cap remain unchanged, solely the volume of demand response measures is increased, from 2 percent of the peak load in the original configuration to 4 percent in the modified configuration used in the scope of the present work. As seen in 2.2, the demand response currently deployed in the French market area amounts to more than 3 GW, thus the change of the parameter is considered to be legitimate by the author.

As a consequence, the long-term electricity price forecasts contain less hours with the price cap setting the price, but the demand response. This leads to a forecast that displays the actual lack of investment incentives provided by the energy-only market and is perfectly in line with the theory. However, in comparison to previous publications using PowerACE and stating the energy-only market is sufficient to guarantee generation adequacy, the energy-only market is not capable of providing sufficient investment incentives to meet security of supply targets, but needs an additional mechanism to foster investments in peak generation capacities. To address that issue, the decentralised capacity mechanism model developed in the scope of the present work will complement the energy-only market and serve as an additional income source for power plants, if there is a future scarcity situation and the energy-only market cannot provide sufficient incentives. However, even with the modified price forecast and the presence of the capacity market, investments are still substantially incentivised through the level of the forecast electricity prices. If the forecast prices are sufficiently high, the capacity certificate price reaches zero, displaying the capacity mechanism is dispensable to incentivise investments. The involved interdependencies and interactions between the energy-only market and the capacity market are however non-trivial, but must be analysed diligently.

4.3. System Boundaries and Input Data

The model developed in this work only considers the French market area. Electricity exchange enters the model by exogenous time series that are based on the net transfer capacities and historical exchanges. The demand evolution is assumed according to the EU roadmap base scenario of the year 2012 (EC 2011). The demand is thus entering the model exogenously and does not adapt as a consequence of the capacity mechanism. The supply side is modelled using power plant data from the World Electric Power Plant (WEPP) data base provided by Platts (Platts 2017). The expansion of installed renewable energies is assumed according to the French national renewable energies action plan (MEEM 2010). The renewable feed-in is determined using the weather time series of the base years 2009 and adapting it to the future installed capacity.

Further, Table 8 provides the investigated investment options and their respective techno-economic parameters. Note, that variable costs are determined with fuel prices and the efficiency of the respective technology. As a fuel price development is assumed according to the EU roadmap base scenario (EC 2011), the variable costs of each technology may change over time.

Table 8: Techno-economic parameters of investment options.

Option	Unit size	Specific Invest-ment	Annual Fixed Costs	Effi-ciency	Lifetime
Unit	MW	€/kW	€/kW	%	years
Nuclear1	1000	2000	42	34	40
Nuclear2	1700	2000	42	36	60
GT	150	400	9	35	35
GT2030	150	400	9	37	35
CCGT small	300	800	18	60	35
CCGT	800	764	18	58	40
CCGT2030	800	729	18	60	40
Hard Coal	800	1300	36	44	45
HC2020	800	1300	36	48	45

4.4. Logic and Implementation of the Capacity Mechanism Model

This subchapter addresses the implementation of the capacity market model into the PowerACE model. The operations related to the mechanism are performed at two different points within the structure of a PowerACE simulation run. A simulation run is generally structured in five steps within the Steps() method, which is the highest level and serves as a simulation schedule. The tick traverses all simulation days in chronological order. Depending on the characteristics of the considered day, the methods performOperationsBeginSim(), performOperationsBeginYear(), performOperationsDay(), performOperationsEndYear() and performOperationsEndSim() are invoked. The first and the latter are invoked on the first and the last simulation day, respectively. If the considered day is the first respective the last day of a simulation year, the methods performOperationsBeginYear() and performOperationsEndYear() are invoked, respectively. The method performOperationsDay() is invoked on each simulation day. This results in the following pseudo code structure:

```
Steps(){

    For (day = 1, day < total days of simulation, day++){

        if(day = first day of year && year = first year){
            performOperationsBeginSim();}

        if(day = first day of year) {
            performOperationsBeginYear();}

        // spot market executed for each day in hourly resolution
        performOperationsDay();

        if(day = last day of year) {
            performOperationsEndYear();}

        if(day = last day of year && year = last year) {
            performOperationsEndSim();}

    }

}
```

Due to the available information and data structure, some preparatory calculations can be carried out prior to the market procedure itself and are implemented in the method performOperationsBeginSim(). The procedure of the French capacity mechanism and its related investment appraisal is invoked at the end of each year in the method performOperationsEndYear(). In the following, the operations performed in the two methods are described in detail. In addition, for the comprehension of readers not familiar with PowerACE, the operations performed in the other three methods are described detailed as well.

Beginning of the Simulation:

At the beginning of the simulation, the initialisation of all capacity auctions for the simulation horizon is performed such that any information related to a capacity auction in a year can be stored to it whenever it becomes available. For example, the calculation of the reference power for the whole simulation period can be performed prior to any market operations for the entire simulation. Since the demand evolution and the security factor are determined exogenously and the reference power is only depending on these two, the reference power can be calculated for the whole simulation period prior to the other simulation operations.

The future annual peak loads are taken from the database and discounted for each year with the security factor, which is defined in the settings given via xml. In the reference configuration, the security factor is set to 0.93 in accordance with RTE's determination for the first four delivery years. The reference power for each year is stored in an array.

Depending on the reference power, the capacity obligations of the obligated parties, i.e. the demand for certificates, are determined. As the exact share of each supply company and large consumer obligated to the capacity mechanism is not known, a certain share of the reference power is assigned to each obligated party. Since there is no strategy differentiation among the obligated parties, the share of each obligated party does not change the results. The capacity obligation for the entire simulation period for each obligated party is stored in a separate array (capacityObligation).

The future expansion of renewable energies enters the simulation model exogenously, too, and is known already for the entire simulation period. Thus, the calculation of the amount of certificates granted to renewables can be performed at the beginning of the simulation. In the model, renewables are taken into account using respective capacity credits for each technology. In the reference configuration, both onshore and offshore wind are assumed to have an availability of 20 percent in the peak period, whereas photovoltaic capacity is assumed to have an availability of 5 percent in the peak period. The capacity credits for wind and photovoltaic are 0.2 and 0.05, respectively. The installed capacity per technology is taken from the market area's renewable energy manager, discounted by the respective capacity credit and then summed to obtain the total reliable renewable capacity for each simulation year. The annual values are stored in the array reliableRenewableCapacity. The method createCertificatesRenewables in CapacitySupplyTrader takes the reliable available capacity coming from renewables and adds a certificate to the HashMap reCertificates for each year. This is then added to the capacity auction of the respective year. The offer price of the renewables' certificate are set to zero as no economic assessment is undertaken to renewables.

Beginning of the Year:

In the performOperationsBeginYear() method, the list of plants available in the respective year is updated as well as techno-economic parameters and market settings that change over time. However, this method was not changed for the capacity mechanism model and is only mentioned for completeness.

Operations on each Day:

In the performOperationsDay() method, among others the spot market is performed. As described in section 4.1, the hourly bids are collected from all suppliers for each generation unit and the supply is matched with the residual demand to obtain the spot market price for each hour of the day. However, no operations specific for the capacity mechanism are performed in this part of the simulation.

End of the Year:

After the operations conclude, which are performed throughout the run of a simulated year, at the end of each simulation year t, the method performOperationsEndYear() is invoked. In this method the decentralised capacity market and the investment planning is executed. It represents the core of the capacity mechanism model. Prior to the operations specific for the present work, carbon certificates trading is performed and the past year's electricity market results are summarised and logged.

The French capacity mechanism is then performed in four steps in year t. Firstly, an electricity price forecast for the years t+4 to t+23 is performed, i.e. 20 years. Second, a central capacity certificate price forecast for the same period is performed. The two generated forecasts are available to all investment planning agents, thus there is equality of information. In the third step, based on the forecasts the investment planners of the supply companies perform their investment decisions for power plants being operational in year t+4 and the plant database is updated. In the fourth step, the capacity market for the auctioned period t+4, i.e. the delivery period, is set up and executed. See Figure 14 for an illustration of the model logic. After the market logic terminates, the results are logged. In the following subchapters, each of the three steps is described in detail.

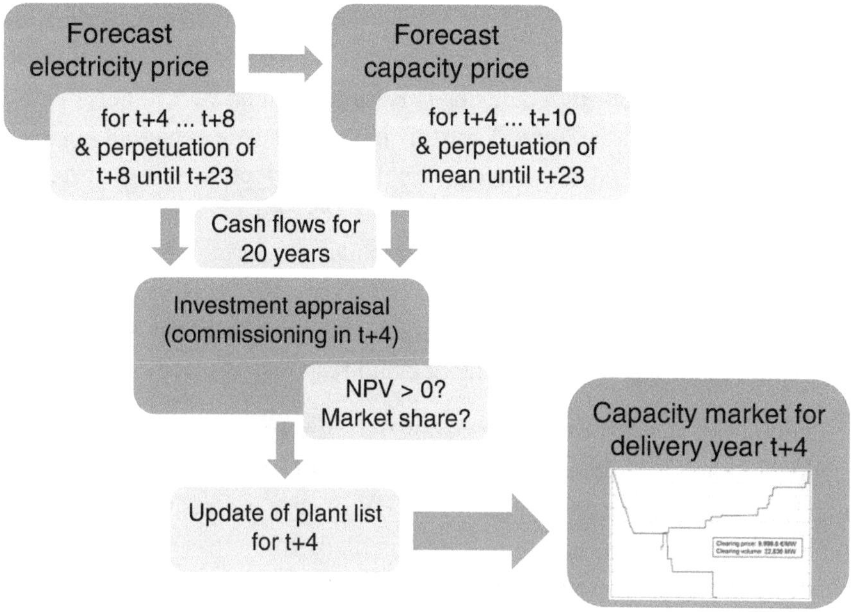

Figure 14: Logical structure of capacity market model.

Step 1: Electricity Price Forecast

To be able to assess investment options, the investment planners require an estimate for the income and the resulting cash flows for the option under consideration. For this purpose, an electricity price forecast for the first 20 years of operation is generated in hourly resolution. This forecast is obtained using a merit order approach. Using the plant park of the respective future year, i.e. plant shutdowns caused by the limits of the technical lifetime are respected as well as an availability for each technology, the future merit order is built for each hour with variable costs as supply bids. Then, the future residual demand is matched with the supply curve to obtain the price forecast for each hour.

However, due to expected shutdowns and a possibly increasing demand, there are scarcity hours. These occur when the supply cannot satisfy the demand. In this case, two measures are considered to avoid a scarcity situation leading to the price cap being the price determinant. First, the exchange with neighbouring countries is reconsidered and set to zero, if the time series foresaw a net export for this hour. This is acceptable, because it is unlikely that based on an economic decision electricity is exported to neighbouring market areas in a real-world scarcity situation. It thus respects the flaw of considering only exogenous time series for exchanges in the forecast. Second, sheddable loads are taken into account to respect a demand response for the scarcity situation. If the demand response enables the market to clear, the price of the demand response is price setting.

Depending on the setting of the parameters for volume and price of the sheddable loads, the appearance of the price cap can be avoided. As seen in 2.1, there are currently roughly 3.5 GW of demand response active in the French market area and the volume is likely to increase slightly in the future (RTE 2017b). In the reference configuration the volume of demand response is set to four percent of the peak demand with a price of 300 € per MWh. These two parameters, however, strongly influence the price forecast and as well the capacity certificate price forecast, as will be explained in the following sections. Thus, sensitivity analyses need to be conducted to display the uncertainty related to the parameters of demand response. If the demand cannot be satisfied despite the reconsideration of the electricity exchange and the consideration of demand response, the forecast price for the hour is set to the price cap of 3000 € per MWh.

As future shutdowns are respected in the price forecast but new investments are not, it is not feasible to execute a price forecast with the described approach for the complete investment horizon. This is because the decreasing installed capacity leads to an increasing number of scarcity hours, thus very high electricity prices and many realisations of the price cap. To obtain a feasible price forecast, the described approach is performed for the year t+4 to t+8, i.e. for the first five years. For the remaining 15 years or until t+23, the price forecast of t+8 are perpetuated. However, this may appear as being too simplified to generate the price forecast for the remaining period. However, as in the net present value approach the later years are less decisive than the first years and other, possibly dynamic, approaches as well appear to contain flaws, the applied approach is considered acceptable and workable.

Step 2: Capacity Certificate Price Forecast

After the electricity prices are forecasted for the entire investment horizon in hourly resolution, the prices for the capacity certificates throughout the investment horizon, i.e. for the years t+4 to t+23, are forecasted by applying a market logic. For this purpose, the demand curve and the supply curve of the future capacity auctions are determined.

Using the forecasted electricity prices and the known future reference power, the capacity certificate prices are predicted by means of the method createPriceForecastFCM(). In this method, using forecasted prices and variable costs of the future generation units, the expected income on the electricity market is estimated for each generation unit on a yearly basis. In each year-loop, the existent plants of the respective year are considered. As in the electricity price forecast, only shutdowns caused by reaching the end of the technical lifetime are considered while additional capacities through new investments or shutdowns for economic reasons are neglected.

To generate the supply curve, the concept of difference costs is introduced. Difference costs are calculated by the following formula for generation unit i in year t:

$$C_{diff,i,t} = max\{0,\ I_{ann,i,t} + C_{fix,i,t} - CF_{markets,i,t}\} \text{ in [€/MW]},$$

with annualised investment payment $I_{ann,i,t}$, the annual fixed costs $C_{fix,i,t}$ and the cash flow generated on markets $CF_{markets,i,t}$. Note that both electricity and balancing energy can be considered here.

The difference costs are defined as the gap between the yearly income and the required income to determine generation unit profitability. If a plant, which cannot cover its investment payment and fixed costs by contribution margins earned on the electricity market, receives a payment in the amount of its difference costs, it only breaks even. The concept of difference costs is often synonymously used with the term “missing money”. However, the term missing money was originally created to describe the missing revenues for peak power plants resulting from the introduction of artificial price caps which are lower than the value of loss load (VoLL) and lead to underinvestment and welfare losses. To be precise, in the present work the terms difference costs and missing money are unique, as the difference costs capture the gap to profitability for all generation technologies. In this sense, a nuclear power plant can also have difference costs, if the contribution margins generated on the markets are not sufficiently high. If the cash flow exceeds the investment payment and the fixed costs, the difference costs are set to zero, as not no negative bids can be expected.

Petitet (2016) describes the difference between “short-term missing money” and “long-term missing money”. Whereas the long-term missing money in her work includes both investment payments and fixed operation and maintenance costs, the short-term missing money only includes the annual fixed operation and maintenance costs. The difference costs elaborated and used in the present work are equivalent to the “long-term missing money” in the sense of Petitet (2016).

For each generation unit in each hour of the year, the variable costs and the forward price are compared to predict the income in the considered year. Afterwards, for each plant the difference costs are calculated for the considered year and a certificate with the difference costs as respective offer price is created. However, it has to be considered that not the entire installed capacity of the plant is granted certificates, but only the share of available capacity. Thus, the calculated difference costs are divided by the capacity factor to obtain a feasible and consistent bid. The volume of the certificate equals the installed net capacity multiplied with a technology-specific capacity factor to respect availability constraints.

The created certificates are afterwards ordered by offer price. The certificate for the renewable capacities, which was already determined in the beginning of the simulation for each simulation year, is added to the list of capacity certificates with a bid price of zero. The demand side is considered to be price-taking and asks for certificated in amount of the reference power for the respective year. In a simplified market procedure, the capacity of the certificates in the list are subtracted one by one from the reference power of the considered year, until the reference power reaches zero. The last capacity certificate required to match the reference power is considered the price-setting one. Thus, the capacity price forecast for the considered year is set to the offer price of the latter.

However, since investors are expected to not over-estimate their future incomes, the forecast price is assumed to be capped at the half of the administrative price cap. If the reference power cannot be matched with the certificates available in the respective year or the bid price of the last required certificate exceeds the half of the administrative price cap for the considered year, the price will be set to the half of the administrative price cap. In the transitory phase of the real-world capacity mechanism, the administrative price cap is 20,000 €/MW in the auctions for delivery year 2017, 40,000 €/MW for delivery years 2018 and 2019 and 60,000 €/MW for delivery year 2020. Traversing the loop for all considered years, when the method terminates the array with capacity price forecasts is filled and returned.

Applying the described approach for the entire investment horizon is not feasible, because the lack of installed capacity due to shutdowns leads to reaching the price cap in all the later years which results in an overestimation of the capacity prices. As future shutdowns were respected in the electricity price forecast but no new investments, the time series of electricity prices that enters the capacity price forecast is basically the forecast for the years t+4 to t+8 and afterwards the prices of t+8 are perpetuated. To not only respect the influence of power plant shutdowns on the electricity prices but also the influence of the shutdowns on the actual capacity market, an approach using the arithmetic mean is applied. Since due to shutdowns the installed capacity is not sufficient to satisfy the certificate demand, the capacity price forecast for the remaining 13 years of the investment horizon is calculated as the arithmetic mean of the forecast prices of the first seven forecast years. In this way, the dynamic nature of the power plant park evolution is respected and a feasible capacity certificate price forecast is obtained. The resulting formula is as follows:

$$p_{certificates,\ year}^{forecast} = \begin{cases} c_{diff,marginal\ unit,year}, & for\ year \in (t+4,\dots,t+10) \\ \frac{1}{7} * \sum_{j=t+4}^{t+10} c_{diff,marginal\ unit,j}, & for\ year \in (t+11,\dots,t+23). \end{cases}$$

As a consequence the decommissioning of power plants is respected in both the electricity price forecast and the capacity price forecast and a time series of prices for the 20 years of the investment horizon is obtained. The investment planners use this capacity price forecast to evaluate their investment options. However, for new investments the first forecast year is crucial since the initial contract lasts seven years and accounts for the main share of capacity revenues considered in the investment appraisal.

Step 3: Investment planning

Following the forecasts for electricity and capacity prices, in a third step the investment planning is performed. For that purpose, each supply company has an investment planner agent which has several investment options at its disposal. The investment options in PowerACE contain nuclear, hard coal, lignite, gas combined cycle and gas turbine power plants. The techno-economic parameters for each option are loaded from the database and consist of among others, specific investment, yearly fixed costs, installed capacity, efficiency and lifetime. In the scope of this work lignite is excluded as an option for the French market area. In addition, EDF is the only supplier in the French market area operating nuclear power plants and thus the only company with sufficient knowledge and experience to commission new nuclear plants. To respect this, the investment planner of EDF is the only one with the nuclear investment option at its disposal. Another constraint related to nuclear power is the capacity cap, that was stated in the Energy Transition for Green Growth Act in 2015. According to this legislation, the installed nuclear capacity must not exceed the currently installed level of 63.3 GW (MEEM 2015). This constraint is respected in the simulation.

The investment options are assessed by each investment agent using the electricity and capacity price forecasts for the investment horizon of 20 years. The net present value is calculated for each option, assuming the investment turns operational in t+4. This is, however, a simplification, as each technology cannot be assumed to have a planning and construction period of only four years. If the option's net present value is positive, the expected future market share of the planner's company is checked. If the company needs to add capacity to keep the market share constant and there is a profitable investment option, the planner decides to add the investment option to the company's portfolio. The different investment planners are hereby invoked in a random order and then execute the method performInvestmentDecision().

In this method, the entire evaluation of possible investment decisions by the respective planner is performed. In the beginning, the existing plants are checked and each plant with very low profits in the previous years and a remaining lifetime of less than five years is logged. In the next step, the planner obtains a list containing all available plant options for the next year and removes straight away those options, which are already assessed as unprofitable by other investment planners or not in line with the regulatory framework. At this point, the nuclear cap is respected.

For each planner, the variable builtCapacity is initialised to record the investments in each period and as well to control that the investments are not factitiously high. In that sense, EDF can only add a maximum of 2.5 GW of capacity per period until 2025, after which the cap is relaxed to 3.5 GW per period to enable an adequate replacement following nuclear decommissioning. For the other investment planners, the investment cap is set to 800 MW per year, to respect financial and human resource limitations. However, these constraints are not limiting in the beginning of the simulation period but ensure that the replacement of nuclear capacity decommissioning from 2025 onwards is modelled in a realistic manner.

As the planner tries to maintain its market share in the future, before the investment appraisal the gap between his current market share and the future share without further investments is calculated. The objective of the planner is thus to close the gap with profitable investment options. After the initialisation of a hash map with unprofitable capacity options of the current investment planner, the capacity options' evaluation begins. In the current version of PowerACE the evaluation of all options is set out at once and implemented in an integrated method. Following this, the approach used for the present scope is presented and explained. Note, that the approach is not changed substantially compared to the original method, but some extensions were added to adapt the method to the case with a decentralised capacity mechanism in France.

After the initialisation of the variables for yearly profit, power profit (i.e. the revenues from electricity sales), emission costs, fuel costs and for the total profit, total power profit, total emission costs and total fuel costs, a loop traversing all investment options one by one is started. In this context, the term "total" describes the discounted sum over the entire investment horizon. In the investment options loop, using the forecasted hourly electricity prices and variable costs, the potential profit of the option is evaluated. At the end of each year the profit, power profit, emission costs and fuel costs are discounted with the discount factor and added to the respective “total” variable. After the last year of the investment period is traversed, the variable for the total profit contains the discounted sum of cash flows, i.e. the net present value, from the electricity market. Note, that the electricity market is considered the only marketing option for the electricity produced by the investment option. A possible participation in balancing energy markets is left out in the present work.

In addition to the profits on the electricity market, in the French market design with the decentralised capacity mechanism, generation capacities generate additional revenues by selling their capacity certificates. To respect this, after the calculation of the total electricity profit, expected revenues on the capacity market throughout the regarded investment horizon are evaluated. For this purpose, the method calculateRevenuesFCMNew() was created and is invoked within the loop of capacity options. The method returns the sum of the discounted capacity market revenues of the capacity option for the specified investment horizon. Therefore, the capacity certificate price forecast generated previously is used for each year. The certified capacity of the investment option is calculated by multiplying the installed capacity with the technology-specific availability factor.

A characteristic of the French capacity mechanism’s market design that is respected in the investment appraisal, consists of the initial contracts for new investments, lasting seven years and guaranteeing the investor capacity certificate prices according to the following formula.

$$contract\ price\ in\ year\ t{:}\quad p^t_{contract} = max\left(p^1_{capacity\ market}, p^t_{capacity\ market}\right)\quad for\ t < 7,$$

with the clearing price of the initial auction of the new investment’s certificates $p^1_{capacity\ market}$ and the clearing price of the auction in the current year $p_{capacity\ market}^{t}$. Note, that in the real-world mechanism the market reference price, i.e. the weighted average of all auctions for delivery year t, is used instead of the price of a single auction. As the model developed in the present work considers only one auction for each delivery year, the market reference price and the price of the auction in t are equivalent.

To respect this, the capacity prices considered for the certificate revenues are calculated by the maximum out of the price of the first forecast year and the considered year for the first seven years, i.e. t+4 till t+10. For the remaining 13 years of the investment horizon, i.e. until t+23, the forecast price calculated as described above is taken. The price for the respective year is then multiplied by the certified capacity of the capacity option to obtain the annual revenue. In order to calculate the net present value of the capacity option including the capacity market cash flow, the net present value of the capacity market revenues, i.e. the cash flow, is added to the net present value of the yearly cash flows, which was stored in the variable for the total profit. Conclusively, the formula for the net present value of the investment option is a follows:

$$NPV_{option} = \sum_{i=t+4}^{t+23} \frac{(-I_i^{ann} - C_i^{fix} + CF_i^{electricity\ market} + CF_i^{capacity\ market})}{(1+IR)^{i-t-3}},$$

with I_i^{ann} the investment payment annualised with the annuity factor, C_i^{fix} the yearly fixed costs, $CF_i^{electricity\ market}$ the cash flow generated on the electricity market in the considered year i, $CF_i^{capacity\ market}$ the cash flow generated on the capacity certificates market in the considered year i and IR the interest rate, set to 0.08 as the standard value.

It can be argued that the forecasted price is not the price, with which a new investment offers its certificates. Considering the risk of being the marginal unit or not being contracted via the capacity market, the best-strategy bid of the new certificate should be incrementally below the forecasted certificate price, thereby guaranteeing the contraction and as well not risking the additional revenues, since the auction is a single-price auction. However, to use the forecasted price in the investment appraisal is acceptable as the probability to significantly alter the capacity price with the new market entry is relatively low.

After each capacity option of the loop is traversed, the list of all capacity options is ordered by the net present value, so that the most profitable capacity option is selected as the best choice. In the next step, the actual investment decision is taken. Using the gap required to close to maintain the market share, the investment planner decides whether there is a need to invest in new capacity or not. If the gap is zero or negative, no new capacity is required and the investment planner decides not to invest. If the gap is greater than zero, the most profitable option is selected and assessed. The assessment consists of two steps.

Firstly, the profitability is checked. If even the best capacity option has a negative net present value, none is chosen to invest into. If the best capacity option is profitable, the second assessment step consists of determining the plant size of the option under consideration. For this purpose, the variable containing the remaining gap is initialised with the value of the planner's gap. Whenever an investment is decided, the size of the new capacity gets subtracted from the remaining gap. While the remaining gap is greater than zero and there are profitable investment options, the investment planner decides to invest in new capacities. The preliminary size of the added capacity is calculated as the minimum of the capacity option's unit size, the fixed investment cap minus the already built capacity in this investment decision and the remaining gap. However, only plants greater than the minimum plant size, e.g. set to 100 MW, can be realized. Thus, if the determined size is lower than the latter, a plant of minimum size is constructed.

Whenever the decision to add a plant is positive, the new plant is added to the power plants list of t+4 as well as the capacity certificates for the auctions for the first seven delivery years (i.e. t+4 till t+11) are created. When this occurs, the variable builtCapacity is increased by the unit size and the remaining gap is decreased by the unit size. When the investment agent is done with its investment decisions, the list of unprofitable power plants is updated and the next investment planner can take its investment decision. This logic is continued until all investment planner agents have taken their investment decisions and step three is consequently completed. The last step in the logic of the capacity market model in year t consists of the market setup and execution for the delivery year t+4.

Step 4: Market Execution

After the forecasts and the investment planning, the capacity market is finally set up and executed. The computational agents involved in the market execution are the capacity market operator, the obligated parties and the capacity supply traders. Since in the current version of the capacity market model, the agents asking for certificates all pursue the same bidding strategy and the agents offering certificates all pursue the same bidding strategy, a simplification in the model consists of having only one capacity supply trader, who offers all the certificates of the capacities and one obligated party, who is assigned 100 percent share of the capacity obligation. However, when considering different bidding strategies of both demand and supply side, the capacity market model developed in this work could easily be adapted by adding different capacity supply trader types and different obligated party types each having their own varied bidding strategies. In the scope of this work, the issue of strategy diversification is not addressed, but the supply trader offers the certificates with the difference costs[8] of the underlying generation unit and the obligated party satisfies its demand in a price-taking manner. Thus, there is just one auction for each delivery year

8 Precisely, the difference costs divided by the technology-specific capacity credit.

instead of multiple auctions as seen in the real-world mechanism. However, game-theoretic analyses of different strategies for different types of agents with, e.g. different risk aversion, especially if more than one auction is considered for each delivery period, might prove insightful. This could be addressed in a further development of the present model and future studies.

The market execution consists of three steps. (I) The bids are called and processed, (II) the market is cleared and (III) the market results are evaluated and logged. In the following, these steps are described in detail.

(I) Since the instance of capacity auction was already created in the beginning of the simulation for each year of the simulation horizon, there is no need to create the capacity auction once again. The initialisation consists of storing the auction period (i.e. time lag between auction and delivery of four years) as well as the lists allBids and bidPoints. Subsequently, the bids from all capacity certificate traders are called. For this purpose each instance of capacity trader, i.e. both obligated parties and the capacity certificate supply traders, executes its method callForBidsCapacity(). The latter is implemented for both obligated parties and capacity certificate supply traders separately.

For obligated parties, the bid volume is loaded from the array created in the beginning of the simulation. The bid volume of each obligated party is added to the total demand volume in the respective year, which is stored in the market operator agent. The bid price is set to the price cap to respect the inelastic price-taking character of the demand side. Using bid volume and bid price, the capacity bids for the obligated parties are created and transmitted to the capacity auction.

For the capacity certificate supply traders, the method callForCapacityBids() is more sophisticated. First, the array list for the capacity bids is initialised. Then, the units which will be available in the considered delivery year, are loaded to the two-dimensional array units, where one dimension is used for the supply companies and the other for the individual units. Using the method createCertificates(), the certificates for the generation units in the array are created for the considered year. Two kinds of generation units are distinguished: For capacities, that are already considered for a period of more than one year as they are new investments and for which the certificate was already created for the duration of the initial contract, i.e. seven years, no new certificate is added to the certificates array list of the capacity auction. For capacities, for which no certificate exists for the respective auction, the reliable capacity and the expected difference costs, based on the electricity price forecast for the considered year, are calculated and a new certificate is created and added to the certificates list of the capacity auction. The difference costs of the plant are stored in the certificate in order to determine the offer price in the next step. When all plants are traversed, the list of capacity certificates in the capacity auction consists of the certificates of renewables, which were created and added in the beginning of the simulation, the certificates of recent investments, which were created and added at investment decision and certificates of "regular" existing plants. This list is then traversed and for each certificate a capacity bid is added to the list capacityBids. The array list capacityBids which contains both the bids of the obligated parties and of the capacity supply traders is then returned.

In the following step, the bids are processed. All bids are traversed and checked for their validity. If there are empty bids, bids with negative bid prices or bids with prices above the maximum bid price, they are removed, adjusted to a bid price of zero or adjusted to the price cap, respectively, and an error message is shown. Afterwards, all capacity bids are added to the list bidPoints as bid points, which is used in the market clearing.

(II) The capacity market is designed as a single price auction, for which a clearing algorithm is already implemented in PowerACE due to the electricity spot market. Thus, to clear the market, a regular call market is set up. Using the bid points, the offer and demand curves are built. After the setup, the market is cleared. Besides the market clearing price and the total traded volume, for each bid point the accepted volume is determined. When the method clearMarket() is finished, each bid point contains both the market clearing price and its respective accepted volume.

(III) The last step in the market execution procedure consists of the evaluation of the market results and the logging. First, each trader agent that participated in the capacity auction evaluates the results individually. Currently, the method to evaluate the results for the obligated parties remains empty, but could be used in a further development. For the certificate supply traders, the evaluation method traverses all capacity bids and increases the income of the underlying plants by the received payment and sums up the traded volume and the bid volume. In addition, the total amount of payments for the supply trader is calculated and stored. The variables for the bid volume, clearing price, sold volume and payments are then logged.

After the individual evaluation, the results in terms of total traded volume, market clearing price, the total payments to capacities and amount of renewable capacity certificates are stored in the capacity auction of the respective year. Finally, for each bid in the list of capacity bids, the variables unit ID, name, capacity, difference costs, volume, clearing price and volume remaining are logged.

After the execution of the capacity market and the evaluation and logging of the results, the method performOperationsEndYear() is closed.

End of the Simulation:

At the end of the simulation, the investment activity throughout the entire simulation horizon is summarised in output files and the evolution of the plant park is plotted. In addition, the overall payments received by capacities are calculated and returned.

4.5. State of the Art and own Contribution

This chapter aims at providing the reader an overview over the state of the art related to analyses of the French capacity mechanism. Approaches different from agent-based simulation have been chosen by other studies to analyse the French capacity mechanism and its impacts on the development of the French electricity system. In this section, these different approaches and representative results shall be presented and discussed. These contain an equilibrium model, a mixed-integer optimisation model as well as system dynamics simulation models. In the end, the additional benefit to the field of science provided by the model developed in this work is assessed. Since the French capacity mechanism was implemented only recently, it is a relatively new and fresh topic and there exists only a limited number of previous publications analysing the quantitative impacts on the evolution of the French electricity system. Nevertheless, these publications have to be recognised in order prepare an exhaustive and thorough work. Thus, the studies by UFE and BDEW (2014), Frontier Economics (2014), FTI CL (2016) as well the works of Petitet (2016) and Zimmermann et al. (2017) are presented and discussed.

Parallel to the preparation of this work, the French transmission system operator RTE prepares an impact assessment report of the capacity mechanism, but will unfortunately not be able to publish it before the due date of the present work. The mentioned impact assessment report promises to contain insightful quantitative analyses related to the capacity mechanism, and should be considered in future works.

Already in the years before the preliminary rules of the capacity mechanism were published by RTE in 2014, two studies analysing the impacts of a decentralised capacity mechanism were prepared by UFE and BDEW (2014) and by Frontier Economics (2014).

4.5.1. UFE & BDEW (2014): System Equilibrium Model

The study published by UFE (French Electricity Union) and BDEW (German Association of Energy and Water Industries) uses an equilibrium model and focusses on the impacts of different market designs on the security of supply and the welfare of France and Germany in 2030, considering cross-border effects as well. The power system model of France and Germany "Artelys Crystal Supergrid" developed by Artelys is used to analyse a hypothetical reference plant park in France and Germany for the year 2030. This reference park is obtained by an optimisation approach and assumes perfect information as well as no risk aversion of investors. According to the authors, it is coherent with other studies by ENTSO-E, RTE and the BMWi. However, since the plant park is updated in the approach, the initial seed is not essential to the model outcome. Additionally, a significant expansion of demand response measures in both France in Germany is assumed, leading to demand response measures amounting to 11 GW in 2030 in France.

The analysis consists of comparing three different market designs: an energy-only market in both France and Germany, an energy-only market in Germany and an energy market with capacity mechanism in France as well as an energy market with a coordinated capacity mechanism for Germany and France. In the context of the present work only the second market design is considered, therefore only the logic and results of second market design are presented here.

The approach can be summarised as follows: The reference park is set as the initial state for the system in 2030. It is then assessed over 50 climatic scenarios. The optimal plant dispatch is determined and based on that, the security of supply level and the resulting revenues for each generation technology are calculated, assuming a capacity price of zero. The 50 climatic scenarios are both important for the demand side as there is a considerable temperature sensitivity, and the supply side as the renewable energy feed-in plays a major role in the future electricity systems of France and Germany. In addition to that, the capacity price is updated according to the rule: If the security of supply level is below the set target, "the price is set to the minimal level that would induce an increase of at least one asset's installed capacity" (UFE & BDEW 2014, p. 35). If the security of supply level is above the set target, "the price is set to the minimal level that would induce a decrease of at least one asset's installed capacity" (UFE & BDEW 2014, p. 35). The plant park is then updated by increasing the capacity of the profitable technologies and decreasing the capacity of the unprofitable technologies, thus triggering an evolution towards an equilibrium plant park. The demand for capacity certificates is equal to the supply for capacity certificates at all time, thus the security of supply target is implicitly met.

The result of the analysis is the equilibrium plant park for France and for Germany that meets the security of supply target and has no unprofitable generation units, because the capacity price is set according to the rule mentioned above. The equilibrium capacity price is 33,600 € per MW in France, but is, due to its determination rule, substantially influenced by the underlying security of supply target of three hours LOLE and not a market outcome.

The analysis of the equilibrium park leads to two main conclusions: First, the installed thermal capacity in Germany decreases, when the capacity mechanism in France is active, meaning the cross-border effects are considerable. Second, the peak generation capacity both in France and Germany increases due to the French capacity mechanism, more significantly in France though. Figure 15 shows the resulting coal, CCGT and peaking capacity in the equilibrium park for France and Germany. However, one must bear in mind, that a significant expansion of demand response was assumed. Under more conservative assumptions, more peaking capacity is necessary to reach the security of supply target, possibly increasing the equilibrium capacity price.

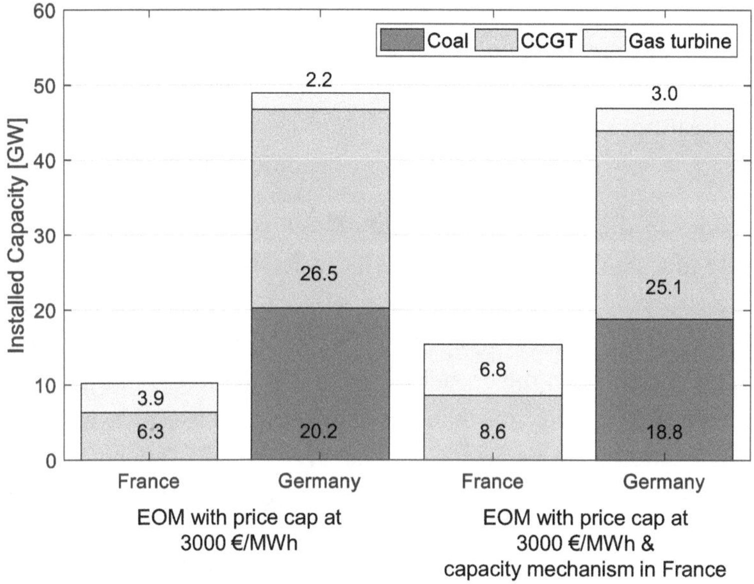

Figure 15: Coal, CGGT and peak capacities in the 2030 equilibrium park, with or without a capacity mechanism in France (UFE & BDEW 2014).

However, several points of the approach need to be discussed. First, the shortcomings of the equilibrium model approach must be mentioned. The model only considers the optimal plant park of one single year, not the development of the system over a period. In reality, investment decisions are however strategic decisions that are taken over time. The plant park is not likely to be as reactive and dynamic as in the equilibrium model, but substantially depends on the existing power plants. The equilibrium power plant determined by the study is thus not the actual plant park that would evolve from a continuous investment behaviour, but a theoretical benchmark towards which a plant park in reality may converge.

Second, even though risk aversion of investors and climatic scenarios are considered, the equilibrium model takes the uncertainty into account insufficiently. Investors have perfect information regarding revenues and the profitability of different technologies, even if the weather uncertainty is captured by the climatic scenarios. In real world investment decisions, uncertainties regarding mid and long term future developments are considered as well, not only the uncertainty of one specific year.

Third, the rules of the French mechanism are not considered sufficiently. The capacity mechanism can be classified as price-based, since prices are set to the level trying to meet the security of supply target and are not a result of a market procedure. Apart from that, no certificates for demand response are considered in the capacity mechanism, whereas in the actual rules of the French capacity mechanism, demand response measures can actively participate in the market. Conclusively, it can be stated that the study published by UFE and BDEW does not serve as feasible benchmark for the model developed in the scope of this work, but only gives a direction to which the electricity system possibly evolves under strong assumptions. Whereas an equilibrium solution can be of great interest for policy makers assessing different market design options or a central planner that takes all investment decision for a system, for an impact assessment an equilibrium model results in an unrealistic solution.

4.5.2. Frontier Economics (2014): Mixed-Integer Optimisation Model

Frontier Economics (2014) investigated the impacts of several market designs containing capacity remuneration mechanisms. The study simulates the investment and decommissioning decisions under different market designs in the market area Germany-Austria with a mixed-integer optimization model, based on an exogenous plant park evolution in other European countries. The plant park evolution is assumed according to the ENTSO-E

Scenario B (ENTSO-E 2013). For France, this leads to a shutdown of 21 GW nuclear capacity until 2035, compensated by an 18 GW expansion of gas-fired plants. Additionally, it contains a further reduction of hard coal compared to 2013. Thus, since no investment decisions and no capacity prices for France are assessed in the scope of the study, it has not the same objective as the present work. However, a decentralised market design is assessed for the German market according to the price-based VKU proposal. Nevertheless, the conclusions as well as the different approach chosen by Frontier Economics might be insightful to the present study as well, thus the study by Frontier Economics is briefly presented at this point.

The mixed-integer optimisation model has the total European system costs as target function and determines the optimal investment decisions for the German market area. In the scope of the study, a comparison of several market designs, particularly one decentralised capacity market design, is performed qualitatively regarding the targets effectivity, efficiency, regulatory policy, cross-border effects.

However, results are not necessarily in favour of the decentralised mechanism. Only in the category effectivity the decentralised mechanism gets a good rating, all other categories are rated neutral by the authors. Conclusively, it must be stated that a mixed-integer optimisation model serves as an alternative approach to the one chosen in the scope of this work. However, Frontier Economics analysed the development of the German market area and did not implement the rules of the French capacity mechanism, but the VKU proposal. Since a different country was the focus of the study and a different mechanism design was assessed, the Frontier Economics study does not serve as a benchmark for the model developed in this work, but only offers an alternative approach for future studies.

Generally, fundamental optimisation models determine an optimal evolution of the system, but are not able to capture the incentives and the behaviour by the market players involved in reality. Further, perfect information about all considered years is already available as of the beginning of the optimisation and thus respected in the optimal solution. Whereas an optimal solution can be of great interest for policy makers assessing different choice options or a central planner that takes all investment decision for a system, for an impact assessment of an existing market design the mentioned points lead to an unrealistic, despite cost-optimal, solution. However, for the institution revising and calibrating the French capacity mechanism, namely RTE, optimisation models are useful and should be applied.

To capture and assess the impact of a capacity mechanism that is already in place, different approaches need to be considered. These approaches simulate investment decisions and the future evolution of the power plant park considering the capacity mechanism as well as market behaviour of the involved market participants. The studies prepared by FTI CL (2016), Petitet (2016) and Zimmermann et al. (2017) meet these needs and are presented and discussed in the following sections.

4.5.3. FTI CL (2016): System Dynamics Simulation Model

The French transmission system operator RTE consulted FTI CL, a French consulting company specialised on energy market analyses, to conduct a study investigating the long-term energy system dynamics and impacts of the capacity mechanism on investments and on neighbouring market areas. FTI CL uses a dynamic modelling approach and simulates the European electricity markets from 2017 to 2040. The modelling approach contains three modules. Using the optimisation platform Plexos, in the first module the optimal power plant dispatch is determined for the existing capacities in each year. The second module consists of a capacity market that is based on the concept of difference costs, which was already introduced in section 0. The third module assesses decommissioning and investment decisions. In all the three modules, there is no diversification of the involved market participants, as perfect competition is assumed.

In a first step, using the security of supply target of three hours LOLE, the volume of the capacity obligation is defined. This step can be compared to the setting of the security factor by RTE. Then the optimal plant dispatch for the considered year and resulting electricity prices are determined. Using these electricity prices, the difference costs for the power plants and consequent capacity market bids in the considered year are calculated. Assuming an inelastic demand for certificates, the volume of the capacity requirement sets the intersection between demand and supply curve on the capacity market, determining the capacity certificate price of the considered year. Based on forecasts for electricity prices, new investment options are assessed for their profitability. Unfortunately, in the FTI CL publication it is not clearly pointed out, whether and to which extent a capacity price forecast for the investment horizon is involved in the investment appraisal. Thus, it must be assumed, that capacity price forecasts are hardly considered, and the investment decisions are taken mainly based on the forecasted energy market revenues. This however does not reflect the capacity mechanisms objective to provide investment incentives to new capacities. After the plant list is updated, the next simulation year is performed with the same model logic, until the end of the simulation horizon is reached.

In addition to the investment options considered in PowerACE and the model developed in the present work, demand response measures are taken into account as investment options. The study assumes 2 GW of demand response potential being cheaply available in the French system in addition to the currently deployed demand response, and roughly 1 GW more demand response potential being available at a higher price. However, the underlying assumptions regarding techno-economic parameters, i.e. mainly the investment, fixed costs and variable costs, of the demand response investment options are not publicly available.

The results of FTI CL show a strong expansion of demand response in the beginning of the simulation period, amounting to almost 3 GW until 2023.

After 2023, when the demand response potential is used up, investments in CCGT and gas turbines are taken. In the long term, compared to a scenario with only the energy-only market, as much as 5 GW of additional available capacity is installed, and financially compensated by the capacity mechanism. See Figure 16 below for the detailed capacity expansion compared to an energy-only market scenario in the long-term.

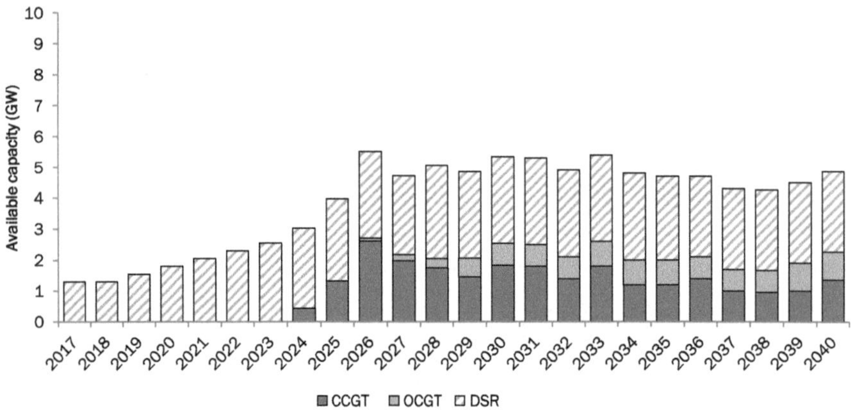

Figure 16: Additional available capacity installed (in comparison to energy-only market scenario) (FTI CL 2016).

The level of resulting capacity prices of the model is shown in Figure 17 below. Whereas in the first years of the capacity remuneration the capacity price remains constantly on a low level of roughly 5,000 € per MW, the prices increase after the deployment of the cheap demand response potential and stabilise around 30,000 € per MW in the long term, which complies with a capacity price increase of factor six in the long term.

The system dynamics simulation model of FTI CL results in a long-term provision of the demanded security of supply target and delivers feasible and desirable results. However, it must be critically reflected to identify possible uncertainties in the results and their extent. The main points of criticism consist of the assumptions regarding demand response, the long-term capacity prices and the related level of security of supply as well as contestable neutrality of the study.

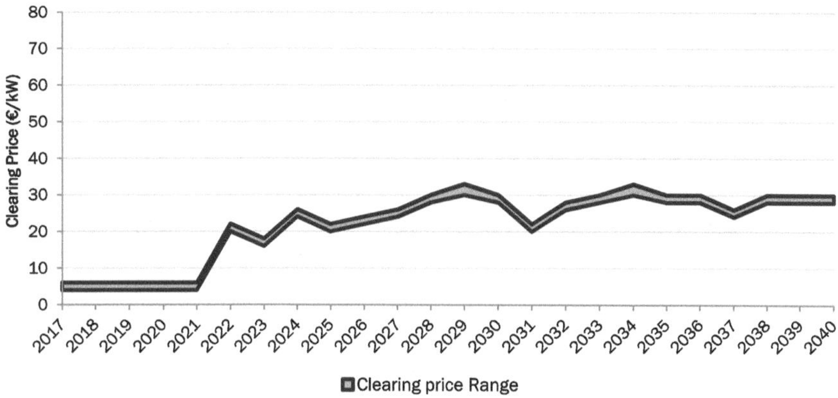

Figure 17: Capacity price development 2017-2040 (FTI CL 2016).

The expansion of cheap demand response is the core result of the study and plays the key role in guaranteeing the security of supply in the system evolution of the study. Thus, the assumption that demand response measures are available in sufficiently amount and at a cheap price, is crucial to the results of the entire study, yet there is no thorough and transparent reasoning for it in the study. However, it would be interesting to see the development of the electricity system with different assumptions regarding demand response in the model of FTI CL. Assuming less potential, a higher investment or higher variable costs for demand response may significantly change the results and conclusions of the study, possibly leading to a larger deployment of gas-fired plants and higher capacity prices in the first years.

The second point of criticism addresses the long-term development of the system. The results contain an additional peak capacity of roughly 5 GW compared to an energy-only market scenario. However, this is mainly depending on the capacity requirement that is determined via the security of supply target of three hours LOLE. As seen in the modelling approach, the capacity market bids are strongly influenced by the revenues of the single generation units on the energy markets. Thus, having capacity prices of 30,000 € per MW in the long term is triggered by a substantial inability of the power plants requested by the capacity obligation level to generate revenues on the energy markets. There is a need to reassess that the model does not over-respect the security of supply target by being too conservative in terms of defining the required capacity to meet the three hours LOLE. Like that, overcapacities can be avoided that are consequently unable to generate sufficient revenues on the energy markets because they are not needed.

One must bear in mind, that prices stabilising on such a high level in the long-term may look desirable and indicate a well-functioning of the mechanism, but result in a payment amounting to three billion € per year, as all certified capacities are paid the clearing price of the single-price auction, and thus to very high system costs. At this point, there is a crucial risk of bad calibration. Thus, the sensitivity analysis with a lower capacity obligation shall provide valuable insights to the uncertainty of the model and result in a lower installed capacity, consequently leading to lower capacity certificate prices and system costs. Unfortunately, this sensitivity analyses, necessary for the validation of the model to have a scientific claim exceeding the one of a consulting company, are not done by FTI CL.

For the model developed in the scope of this work, the system dynamics model of FTI CL does not serve as a benchmark, as the assumptions regarding demand response and a high level of the capacity obligation substantially influence the results. Further, no sensitivity analysis with assumptions similar to the model of the present work is conducted. Thus, the results are hardly comparable.

The last point of criticism is a rather general one and addresses a phenomenon called self-fulfilling prophecy. The study was commissioned by RTE, who is responsible for the market rules and the mechanism parameters. The objective of the capacity mechanism that was a priori known by FTI CL, is to provide incentives for new investments in demand response and peak generation capacities. Fortunately, the impact assessment study concludes, that the mechanism triggers new investments in demand response and peak generation and long-term functioning of the mechanism. Indeed, the study was conducted by an independent consulting company and in all conscience, but the study lacks criticism and critical reflection of the applied approach and the underlying assumptions. The desirable study results are accepted and not challenged sufficiently. To be able to interpret the results thoroughly and to discuss strengths and shortcomings of the methodology, the assumptions should be published in a more detailed manner, especially the assumptions regarding the chosen investment options that are the key driver for the long-term development.

4.5.4. Petitet (2016): System Dynamics Simulation Model

An investigation with a higher scientific claim was published by Petitet in her dissertation, that was a cooperation project of the University Paris Dauphine and RTE. Petitet develops a system dynamics simulation model (SIDES, Simulator of Investment Decisions in the Electricity Sector) assessing the impacts of the French capacity mechanism on investments and the evolution of the electricity system. Thus, the work of Petitet and FTI CL can thus be classified in the same category.

Respecting the rules of the capacity mechanism proposed by RTE, she pursues an approach similar to the approach of the model developed in the scope of the present work. For each simulation year, the power plant dispatch is simulated based on marginal-cost pricing and the difference costs, which she names missing money, are calculated. Based on an electricity and a capacity price forecast, investment decisions are assessed by a representative investor agent. The fact, that there is only one representative investor, respects the assumption of perfect competition. The considered investment options contain a nuclear option, a hard coal option, a CCGT option as well as a gas turbine option and detailed information regarding the techno-economic parameters assumed is provided (Petitet 2016, p. 169). Thus, the investment options considered in SIDES contain the same technologies as the options considered in PowerACE, which makes the results comparable.

However, the initial state of the power system considered in the impact analysis is not the installed capacity in France as of 2017, but a generation park that was determined based on the screening curves method[9] for the French system. It contains a significantly lower share of nuclear plants and a larger share of other thermal capacities (Petitet et al. 2017).

Petitet defines two different plant shutdown cases, one with a model-endogenous and one with an exogenous determination of plant shutdowns. Four different market designs are assessed for both cases: two energy-only markets with administrative price caps of 3,000 € and 20,000 € per MWh and two energy markets complemented with the decentralised capacity market and the security of supply target of 0.5 and 3 hours of LOLE. Additionally, different risk aversion levels are considered in the evaluation of new investments. Using such a thorough and exhaustive experiment design, the interdependencies of the capacity mechanism model parameters are well understood and transparently communicated.

The main conclusions drawn from the model are addressing the effect of risk aversion and the effect of exogenous shocks on the capacity price level. Petitet identifies a significant difference for the cases of an energy-only market and the presence of a capacity mechanism, when risk aversion is included in investment planning. Whereas the energy-only market with a price cap of 3,000 € per MWh is not able to meet the 3 hours LOLE security of supply target, the market designs with an energy-only market with a price cap of 20,000 € per MWh, with a capacity market targeting 3

[9] Method to determine an optimal generation park for a given load duration curve.

hours LOLE and with a capacity market targeting 0.5 hours LOLE are capable of meeting their respective targets. This conclusion holds even under strong risk aversion (Petitet 2016, p. 194).

Further, resulting capacity prices for the simulation horizon 2015 until 2035 are provided as well as the evolution of the model plant park in the long term. See Figure 18 and Table 9 for the quantitative results obtained by system dynamics model. It must be critically reflected, to which extent the obtained capacity prices can be considered a benchmark for the French capacity market. As the term system dynamics model states, the results and identified impacts highly depend on the investigated system. Thus, a model park created artificially by determining the optimal plant park for a given load duration curve is resulting in different system dynamics than a real-world plant park, that historically evolved and is not optimal for a given load duration curve.

To investigate this more thoroughly, the electricity prices and forecasted electricity prices generated by the model park must be compared to the electricity prices and forecasted electricity prices generated by the real-world park applying the same methodology. Deviations in the properties of the price time series have a substantial influence on the resulting difference costs for each generation unit. As the generation units bid into the capacity market with their difference costs, the shape and properties of the electricity prices and price forecasts have as well a substantial influence on the resulting capacity market clearing prices. Consequently, the entire quantitative results provided by Petitet only hold for the initial model plant park that is investigated. To obtain quantitative results, that are valid for the French electricity system and its long-term development, the model must be applied to the real-world plant park as the initial seed.

As the quantitative results are strongly depending on the initial plant park, the conclusions, that can be drawn from the capacity price development, are therefore of rather qualitative nature. The application of endogenous plant shutdowns (for economic reasons) results in a smooth long-term evolution of capacity prices. Further it can be concluded that a higher security of supply target[10] leads to a higher capacity price as more capacity is required, which is according to intuition.

[10] In the sense, that the reliability is higher. A 0.5 hours LOLE target is considered higher than a 3 hours LOLE target.

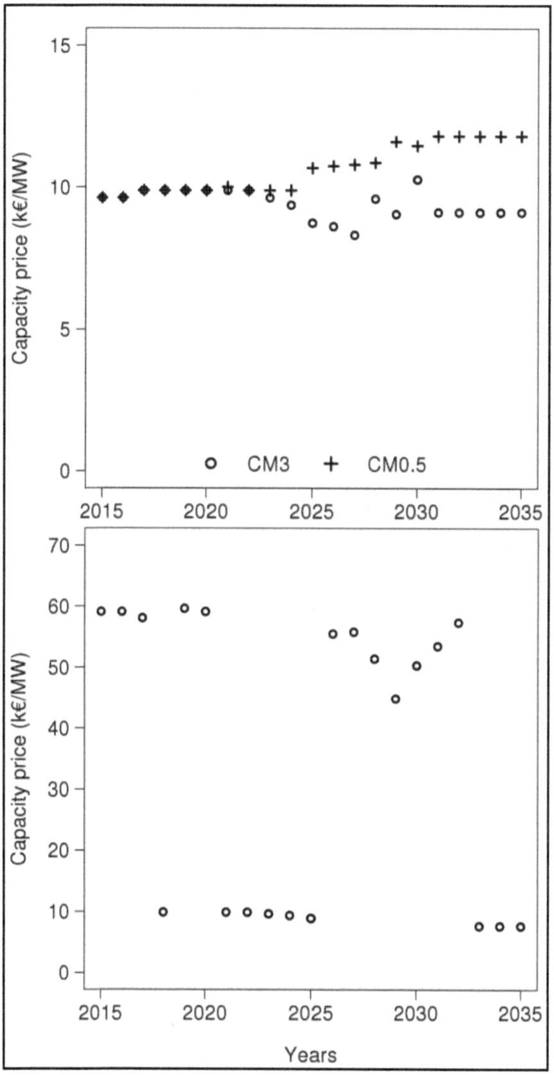

Figure 18: Top: Capacity price evolution with model-endogenous plant shutdowns, security of supply target 0.5 and 3 hours LOLE and no risk aversion of investor (Petitet 2016, p. 180).
Bottom: Capacity price evolution with exogenous plant shutdowns, security of supply target 3 hours LOLE and no risk aversion of investor (Petitet 2016, p. 188).

The application of exogenous plant shutdowns however leads to spikes in the capacity price evolution, as scarcity situations occur as exogenous shocks and the system is not able to anticipate them. When the system reacts to the scarcity and new capacities are commissioned, the capacity price stabilises on a level similar to the result of the endogenous case. However, as a conclusion for the model developed in the scope of the present work, it can be stated that exogenously defined shutdowns may result in a high volatility and spikes in the capacity price evolution.

Interpreting the evolution of the plant park, it must be considered that an expansion of wind power is assumed amounting to an installed wind capacity of 70 GW. This significant change in the electricity system leads to a decreased overall capacity level necessary to meet the security of supply target. However, the endogenous and the exogenous case show significant differences. Whereas in the endogenous case, the base-load technologies nuclear and coal remain in the system and thus economically profitable, in the case of an exogenous shutdown the decommissioned base-load capacity is replaced by mid- and peak-load capacities, namely CCGT and gas turbines. This respects the increasing share of volatile wind feed-in and follows intuition. In both the endogenous and the exogenous case, the presence of the capacity mechanism leads to an increased overall capacity level, especially in the peak-load section.

The work of Petitet developed a consistent methodology that meets the highest scientific claims. The initial plant park used for the capacity mechanism impact assessment however is not the real-world French plant park, but an idealised and artificially created plant park. The quantitative results obtained from the analyses are thus not representative for the French electricity system. The results obtained are desirable and prove the influence of the capacity mechanism on a hypothetical plant park. However, the hypothetical plant park may as well be the reason for the constant capacity prices on a low level, as the prices on the electricity market are closer to theory because of the more diversified merit order. The objective of Petitet is less to analyse the impact on the French electricity system, but to show the general functioning and the impact of the capacity mechanism on investments in a hypothetical system (Petitet 2016). This objective is fully met, but the lack of realism disqualifies the work of Petitet to serve as a benchmark for the present work.

Table 9: Results for model park evolution with endogenous shutdown decisions for the energy-only market with a 3,000€/MWh price cap and the capacity mechanism with a 3 hours LOLE target (left), and exogenous shutdown decisions for the same cases (right) (Petitet 2016).

Installed Capacity [GW]	Seed plant park	Case endogenous, 2035		Case exogenous, 2035	
	2015	EOM3	CM3	EOM3	CM3
Nuclear	43.0	43.0	43.0	33.2	33.2
Coal	20.0	20.0	20.0	11.8	12.5
CCGT	19.0	15.2	14.2	23.3	24.8
Gas Turbine	18.0	10.7	13.1	18.0	19.4
Total non-RES	100.0	88.8	90.3	86.3	89.9

The plant park analysed in the model of the present work is not optimal, but realistic and thus probably does not give out an artefact and desirable price structure. As the electricity prices and their structure substantially influence the dynamic of the system and the results of the simulation, different results must be expected from the own model. These different results may have the shape of more unstable prices and a worse functioning of the capacity mechanism. However, if the impact of the capacity mechanism on the French electricity system of 2017 shall be assessed, the simulation model needs to be run with the existing French generation capacities as an initial seed.

Unfortunately, Petitet did not apply her system dynamics model on the real French data in her publication. Even though the results might have not looked as good as the results of the initial plant park Petitet used, the results would be crucially insightful and valuable to the discussion of both the impacts of the capacity mechanism on the long-term development of the French electricity system and the discussion of the results obtained in this work. The fact that the methodology used by Petitet is similar to the approach pursued in this work however confirms the chosen approach to be sufficiently sophisticated and respecting a high scientific claim.

4.5.5. Zimmermann et al. (2017): Agent-based Simulation Model

As mentioned in section 4.1, Zimmermann et al. (2017) analysed the impact of the implementation of a decentralised capacity mechanism in the French market area using the agent-based simulation model PowerACE. This study was prepared and presented in the context of the IEWT in Vienna 2017[11].

To the knowledge of the author, it is the first impact assessment, that was conducted without RTE being involved. On the one hand, this contains the opportunity to conduct an independent study without expecting results a priori. On the other hand, it contains the risk of not considering important details regarding the mechanism design and thus obtaining results that are not fully representative for the capacity mechanism in the context of the French electricity system. The simulation model for the French capacity market was modelled based on the model of the decentralised capacity mechanism proposal by VKU, that was applied for the German market area in a previous publication by the Institute for Industrial Production and

[11] Internationale Energiewirtschaftstagung (German for: International energy economics conference).

Fraunhofer ISI (Keles, Renz, et al. 2016b). To respect the specific mechanism design and the properties of the French electricity system, some changes were applied. The objective of the publication was to quantify the impacts of the implementation of a capacity mechanism in the French market area on the neighbouring market area, mainly for the Germany-Austria market and the Belgian market.

The structure of the capacity market model is similar to the model developed in this work. Generation units bid into the capacity market with their respective expected difference costs. Based on electricity price forecasts and the past capacity market results, the investment planners take investment decisions. However, the methodology does not consider the capacity mechanism rules in-depth. For example, the demand for certificates is determined by adding a security margin of 2 GW on the expected peak load of the considered year. This leads to a capacity obligation that exceeds the level of the capacity obligation defined by the French mechanism's rules. The certification of generation capacities is not considered thoroughly, but regarding a capacity obligation amounting to the peak demand plus an additional margin, the certification cannot be done according to the French capacity mechanism as the supply and the demand for certificates would not match. Further, the electricity price forecasts were not adapted to respect the need for a capacity mechanism in providing sufficient investment incentives (see chapter 4.2 for a detailed discussion), thus the difference costs tend to be underestimated as the electricity price forecasts contain many scarcity hours reaching the 3000 € per MWh price cap and thus do not reflect the market flaws in reality. Thus, the capacity obligation tends to be overestimated and the supply bids tend to be too low.

As the study was prepared for a conference contribution, it is not exhaustively elaborated and lacks in comprehensiveness. Unfortunately, no key parameters of the modelling are presented and their interdependences are not discussed. However, the results merit to be presented. Zimmermann et al. (2017) obtain an increased investment activity in peak generation from

2032 on, triggered by increasing capacity prices in the mid- and long-term. As illustrated in Figure 19, the capacity prices resulting from the capacity market model are very volatile throughout the simulation period, and show a clear tendency to increase after 2040. However, no convergence towards a focal price level can be observed.

Figure 19: Capacity price development 2020-2050 (Zimmermann et al. 2017).

To conclude, it must be stated that the study does not serve as a benchmark for the present work. Despite being implemented in the same power market model and determining the capacity bids in the same way, the closer investigation shows that the differences between the model by Zimmermann et al. and the model developed in this work outweigh the similarities and the results are thus hardly comparable. The objective of the study was rather to assess effects of the French capacity mechanism on neighboring market areas, both on electricity prices and on the capacity development, than to conduct an exhaustive assessment of the impact on the French market area.

Due to the lack of a model of the French capacity market respecting the mechanism rules as proposed by RTE appropriately, the present master thesis was elaborated and a model of the French capacity market in the PowerACE simulation environment was developed. The following section provides a reflection about how the developed model contributes to the scientific discussion and how it improves the state of the art.

4.5.6. Contribution of the own Agent-based Simulation Model

The capacity mechanism model developed in the scope of this work is a simulation model embedded to the agent-based simulation model PowerACE and thus shows typical characteristics of simulation models. It depicts the behaviour of the different market players and determines the development of the electricity system as a consequence of individual decisions taken by the market players. However, the simulation consists of emulating the real world and does not consider system optimality, thus the obtained results are by far not determining a cost-optimal or welfare-maximising development of the French electricity system, but a development that is likely to happen under the given conditions and assumptions.

The developed model applies a methodology which respects the legislative framework, as expected to be in-state from 2019 on. The methodology is considering both electricity and capacity price forecasts to determine investment decisions by several investment planners. In the current state, it can be compared to the system dynamics model developed by Petitet, which was presented in 4.5.4. Naturally, Petitet considered more aspects and conducted more in-depth analyses in her dissertation. However, Petitet did not apply the system dynamics model to the French case, but to an artificial initial plant park.

In this sense, the present work is the first scientific publication that applies a thorough methodology to the French electricity system and assesses the impacts of the capacity mechanism on the specific French case. One may argue, that the study prepared by FTI CL matches this description as well. In section 4.5.3 of the present work, it was however demonstrated that the results of the mentioned study are strongly depending on the non-transparent assumptions regarding demand response measures and that the study tends to lack in scientific claim, as it was prepared by a consulting company.

Further, it is the first quantitative impact assessment of the French capacity mechanism, that was developed and conducted independently from RTE. Thus no a priori expectations influenced the modelling and the assumptions that were made and the model claims to be neutral towards the outcome. In addition, it offers opportunities for further developments to diversify the bidding strategies on both the demand side and the supply side as it is structured agent-based. So the model not only can be deployed as a system dynamics model, but as well as an agent-based simulation model. However, in the scope of this work no bidding strategies were diversified.

To conclude, the present work is a unique and necessary study. It adds value to the scientific discussion and shall serve as a base for further analyses and impact assessments. Naturally the developed model is not free of shortcomings and flaws. These will be discussed in section 6.

5. Results and Sensitivity Analyses

In this chapter, the results of the capacity mechanism model developed in the scope of this work are presented and discussed. As the key parameters influencing the model results, the security factor, the wind capacity credit and the amount of demand response measures available in the system have been identified.

To be able to thoroughly interpret the interdependencies of the different model parameters, several configurations are simulated and analysed. First the reference case (Ref), applying a security factor of 0.93 and a wind capacity credit of 0.20 as defined by RTE for the first model years. Further, a demand response volume of four percent of the peak load, in accordance with the currently installed demand response measures observed in chapter 2.2. Second the high security of supply (SoS+) case, in which a higher security of supply is targeted compared to the reference case. This is achieved using a higher security factor, resulting in a higher capacity obligation. Further, in the SoS+ case, the installed wind capacity is granted more certificates, as the capacity credit is higher. The demand response amounts to four percent of the peak demand, in accordance with the reference case and the current French system. Finally the SoS- case, in which the security factor is reduced and thus the capacity obligation. However, a lower security factor can not only be interpreted as a reduction the security of supply target by the French government, but as well as a positive impact of a successful European market integration, leading to higher cross-border transfer capacities and thus a higher contribution of the neighbouring countries to the French security of supply. As a consequence, the amount of capacities in the French system needed to meet the present security of supply target is reduced. Thus, the SoS- case shall not be interpreted as a reduction of the security of supply target, but as a reduction of the need to provide security of supply with French capacities. The wind capacity credit is defined to the value proposed by RTE. The demand response in the SoS- case is set five percent, complying with a slight exogenous expansion of demand response compared to the reference case. An overview over the experimental design is provided by Table 10.

The experimental design allows to analyse the interdependencies and influences of the identified key parameters on the results of the model. It as well displays the uncertainty of the model results and thus indicates the uncertainty of the impact of the capacity mechanism on the evolution of the French electricity system. However, none of the cases is meant to predict the exact future development and the exact level of capacity prices until 2050. The objective of the experimental design is to understand the simulation model in-depth and to identify and understand substantial drivers of the future developments and their interrelations. The parameter levels are thus chosen to display the uncertainty and the range of possible results under different assumptions.

Table 10: Experimental design.

Parameter levels in the analysed cases	Unit	Ref	SoS+	SoS-
Security factor	-	0.93	0.96	0.90
Wind capacity credit	-	0.20	0.30	0.20
Demand response	% of peak load	4	4	5

As described in chapter 4.1, the decommissioning of power plants in the model is based on a technical lifetime approach. This means, that whenever a power plant exceeds its technical lifetime, it is shut down. In the wording of the system dynamics model of Petitet described in 4.5.4, the decommissioning is thus entering the model exogenously. However, in the period

2026 until 2042 the simulation logic decommissions roughly 50 GW of nuclear capacity (cf. Figure 1 in chapter 2.1), the shutdowns of other technologies are practically negligible to the system development.

The results presented in the following contain the investment decisions and the evolution of capacity prices. However, the electricity prices and electricity price forecasts are relevant for a thorough interpretation, too. Note, that the prices shown in Figure 20, Figure 22, Figure 23 and Figure 25 correspond to the delivery year, not the year where the auction takes place. In that sense, the point for the year 2020 is obtained with the capacity auction taking place at the end of simulation year 2016. Same applies for the new investments provided by Figure 21, Figure 24 and Figure 26, where the year indicates the year of commissioning, not the year in which the investment decision was taken.

5.1. Reference Case

The reference case complies with the parameter values proposed by RTE. Regarding the capacity price development, which is illustrated in Figure 20, three periods can be distinguished. The first period lasts until 2023, the second from 2024 until 2034 and the third from 2035 until the end of the simulation. In the first two years the price caps of 20,000 and 40,000 € per MW are reached, but in the years 2019 till 2023 the capacity prices drop significantly. From 2024 on, the prices rise again and reach the price cap for several consecutive years and remain on a high level until 2034. In the third period, prices drop to zero again and rise again towards the end of the simulation.

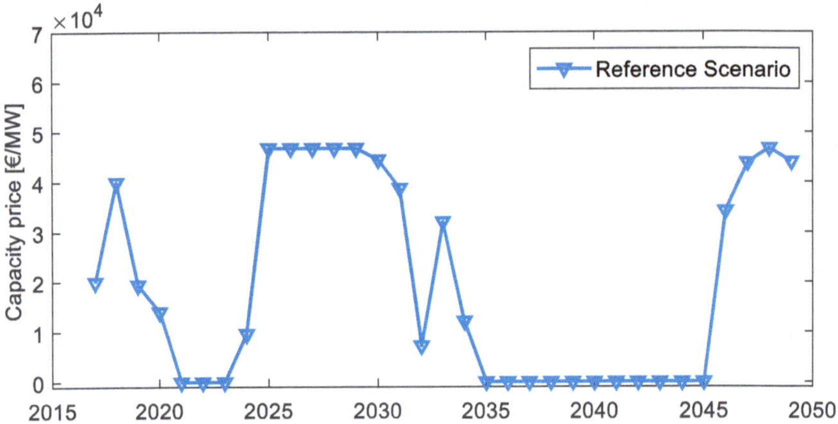

Figure 20: Capacity price development in the reference case.

The investments in the reference case follow a clear pattern, as shown in Figure 21. In the first years, there is barely any investment activity. In the years 2023 until 2028, a significant amount of 14.4 GW of gas-fired power plants is commissioned, starting with gas turbines in the years 2023 and 2025, followed by CCGT in the years until 2028. After 2028, nuclear capacity is commissioned strongly for eleven consecutive years. The amount of nuclear capacity commissioned in each year is mainly determined by the investment cap implemented in the investment planning and respects limited practical construction resources in reality. However, one conclusion which can be drawn from the investments is that the nuclear capacity decommissioned from 2026 on is not replaced completely by new nuclear power plants, but as well by CCGT, and in the long term by gas turbines. This respects an adaption of the electricity system towards a more flexible system, anticipating more fluctuant electricity prices and a lower base load level, because the residual load does not contain a classical base load band, but is characterised by a large share of renewable energies in the system.

To interpret the results, it must be reflected how the investment decisions and capacity prices can be explained. An in-depth understanding of the developed simulation model is required to explain the interdependencies of the different model elements and how they interfere in the determination of the results. The key model elements that will be analysed in the following

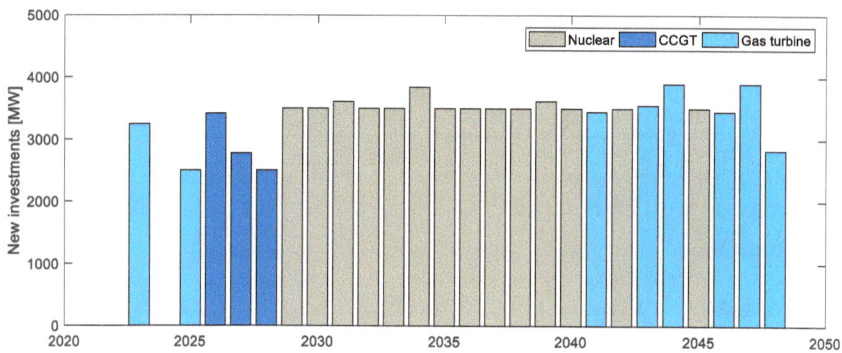

Figure 21: New investments in the reference case.

are the price forecasts and their changing characteristics throughout the simulation horizon, the model-exogenous plant shutdowns and renewable energy expansion, the techno-economic parameters of the power plants as well as the security factor defining the capacity obligation.

The capacity price development is substantially driven from the supply side by the installed plants and the electricity price forecasts. Whereas the demand side is buying price-taking in the amount of the capacity obligation, the supply side determines the capacity bids for each generation unit, based on the expected income on the electricity market. As a result, the capacity bids are driven by the expected income, the annual fix costs and the annual investment payments. The capacity prices in the beginning of the simulation period can be explained by low expected income for generation units that are requested by the capacity obligation. To show, that the price cap is not reached because of an undersupply of capacity, a simulation run of the reference case with inactive price cap was consulted. As indicated by Figure 22 the capacity prices obtained from that run are not essentially above the administrative price cap in the first years and there is sufficient capacity in the system to meet the capacity obligation.

In the following years, the capacity prices are on a low level, meaning the expected electricity market cash flow of the generation units is sufficient to cover the fix costs and the investment payment. For the years after 2023, the shutdown of power plants, which is exogenously defined by the technical lifetime, essentially influences the electricity price forecast and consequently the capacity price forecast. The slightly increasing demand over time may as well be a driver here, but is not further considered in this interpretation.

The increasing overall level and the increasing appearance of price cap hours in the electricity price forecast, which serves as an indicator for the future scarcity, leads to investment planners investing in new capacities. The capacity price forecast, which is capped at the half of CONE, represents an additional investment incentive, especially for technologies with low fixed costs and low investment payments. However, if there are sufficient capacity certificates available to meet the capacity obligation, the capacity price forecast is negatively correlated with the increasing electricity prices and the appearance of price cap hours. Whereas if the amount of capacity certificates available is expected to not be sufficient to meet the future capacity obligation, the capacity price forecast provides a further investment signal in addition to the increased electricity price forecast level. In that sense, the scarcity caused by the rapid shutdown of several GW of nuclear capacity per year (see Figure 1, chapter 2.1) between 2027 and 2037 is displayed more transparently by the capacity market and appropriate investment incentives are given to the investment planners.

As the investment decisions are based on an investment horizon of 20 years, in the first years after commission the added generation units are not necessarily profitable[12]. As can be seen in Figure 22, the generation units required to meet the capacity obligation have difference costs exceeding the capacity price cap by far. The price-setting generation unit has difference costs above 100,000 € per MW in the hypothetic capacity auctions without price cap of 2026 till 2031. In the actual capacity auctions, these bids are corrected downwards to the CONE.

As a thorough analysis of the simulation data shows, these price-setting units are the nuclear power plants, both newly built and existing. The high expected difference costs in these years are caused by two main reasons: The increasing influence of renewable energies decreasing the overall electricity price levels and the newly commissioned gas-fired peak load plants leading to vanishing price cap hours and hours where demand response sets the price in the electricity forecast. As a consequence, the electricity price forecast is on a low level and the existing nuclear power plants are unable to generate sufficient contribution margins to cover their fixed costs and investment payments[13].

---

12 One may think of an exemplary generation unit, which is expected to be unprofitable in the first years, but promises to compensate the negative cash flows of the first years with higher cash flows in the later years. It is the base of the net present value approach, that the net present value over the entire investment horizon can be positive despite having negative cash flows in the beginning. High electricity price forecasts for the later years can serve the planners as a promise for cash flows compensating the negative cash flows of the first years and lead to investments, which are unprofitable in the beginning of their lifetime.

13 The increased capacity prices from 2046 on are due to further plant shutdowns expected in the years 2047 to 2049, leading to a similar situation as from 2025 on. The scarcity was anticipated by the investment planners, which invested in additional gas-fired power plants. The surplus of installed capacity leads to unprofitable generation units and thus to increased difference costs.

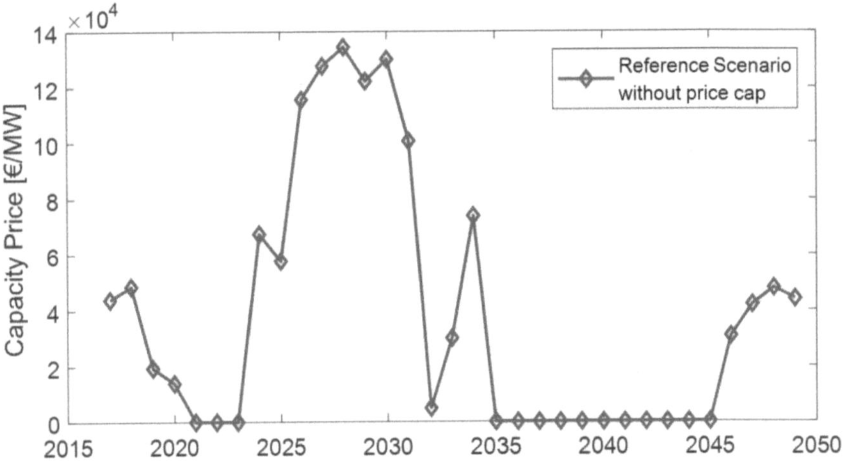

Figure 22: Capacity price development in the reference case without respecting the price cap.

In must be emphasised, that the overcapacity is not mainly triggered by an overestimation of the expected capacity prices. In the investment appraisal, the forecasted capacity prices are capped at half of the CONE. The new investments are therefore mainly based on the high electricity price forecasts for the following years, when the old nuclear plants leave the market. This conclusion can be confirmed by the investments in nuclear power plants and gas turbines in the later years that take place even at a capacity price level of zero.

When a sufficient amount of decommissioning took place, the capacity prices after 2035 drop to zero. This indicates, that the entire power plant fleet requested by the capacity obligation is able to be profitable on the electricity market alone. Thus, the capacity market is no longer necessary to guarantee the profitability of the peak power plants. In this sense, the capacity market enables the plant fleet to develop into a period, in which all power plants generate sufficient revenues and the security of supply is guaranteed, indicated by the fact that the capacity obligation can be met and sufficient certificates are on the market.

The capacity mechanism in combination with the expectation of a future scarcity situation generate sufficient investment incentives to guarantee the security of supply in the long term. The future scarcity is hereby indicated more transparently because of the capacity mechanism and additional revenue streams that are particularly triggering investments in peak power plants.

The overall capacity payments from the obligated parties to the generation units amount to 47 billion € until 2050. However, this value must be challenged. On the one hand, the price cap is reached in many years, which may lead to an overestimation of the overall payments. New investments commissioned in the years with price cap are granted initial contracts for difference last seven years, causing high costs to consumers. On the other hand, the capacity price drops to zero in many years as well, which may lead to an underestimation.

To conclude the interpretation of the reference case results, it can be stated that the market design with a functioning electricity market complemented by a capacity mechanism is able to provide the security of supply and that the demand for capacity certificates can be satisfied at all time. Thus, the capacity market is effective. To which extent it is cost-efficient and welfare-maximising needs to be discussed further. As pointed out in chapter 4.5, there is a lack of comparable benchmarks for the simulation model. The level of the capacity prices and the resulting capacity payments of 47 billion € can therefore hardly be classified as too high or too low, but must be regarded and interpreted as the outcome of the present simulation model. For a better understanding of the model and a reflection, the following chapters provide simulation results for different parameter configurations to identify key factors and their interdependencies in the developed model.

5.2. SoS+ Case

The SoS+ case was defined to analyse the impact of a higher security factor and a higher capacity credit of wind power on the investments and capacity prices. The results will not be interpreted as thoroughly as the results of the reference case, however many of the interplays identified in the chapter before analogously apply for this case. The focus shall be set on the differences between the SoS+ case and the reference case.

Regarding the capacity prices, a similar development as in the reference case can be observed (Figure 23). In the first years, the price caps are reached, followed by a period of low capacity prices. In the course of new investments based on the forecasts, after 2024 the capacity prices reach the price cap for several consecutive years, and are then dropping to zero after 2035. In the end of the simulation horizon, capacity prices rise again, but do not remain on a constant high level as in the period 2024 to 2035.

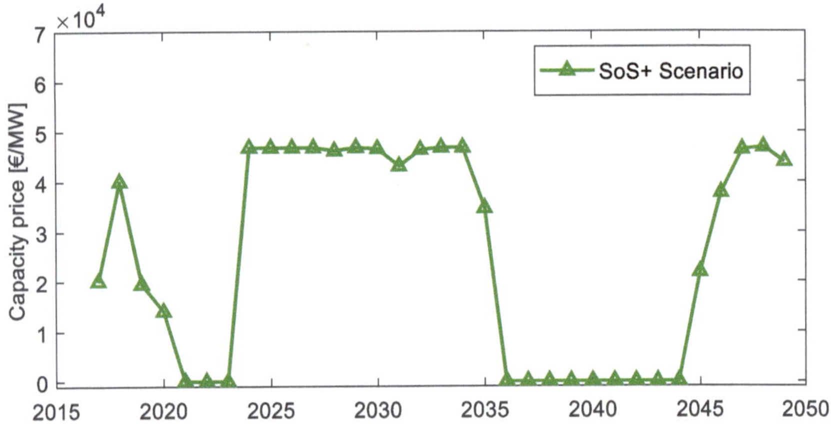

Figure 23: Capacity price development in the SoS+ case.

The investments too show a similar pattern, with a commissioning of gas-fired power plants until 2028, followed by investments in nuclear plants until 2041 (see Figure 24). In the long-term, further investments in gas turbines take place. However, to identify the impact of the changed capacity mechanism parameters on the provision of investment incentives, a focus is set on the investments until 2028. Compared to the reference case, where 14.4 GW of gas-fired plants were commissioned, in the SoS+ case 17.0 GW of gas-fired plants are added, complying with a difference of 2.6 GW. This represents a significant change in the investments, triggered by an increased capacity obligation. Thus, the system resulting from the SoS+ case has a higher level of security of supply compared to the reference case.

The capacity prices are on a similar level in the first simulation years. The interpretation of the period of high capacity prices is analog to the reference case presented in the previous chapter. However, the period of high capacity prices lasts longer and is more stable than in the reference case. Combined with an increased level of capacity in the system, this results in higher overall payments from the obligated parties to the generation companies. The calculated capacity-related payments until 2050 amount to 66 billion € in the SoS+ case, thus by far exceeding the payments of 47 billion € calculated for the reference case.

The difference is even weakened by the additional certificates that are granted to wind power. However, the influence of the different consideration of wind power is relatively low, as it affects only the capacity price and thus counteracts the increased security factor to some extent. In that sense, in the auction logic the increase of the wind capacity credit for the simulation model is equivalent to a provision of additional certificates for the obligated parties to reduce their capacity obligation. Nevertheless, the capacity price as the outcome of a single-price auction must be paid for the additional certficates.

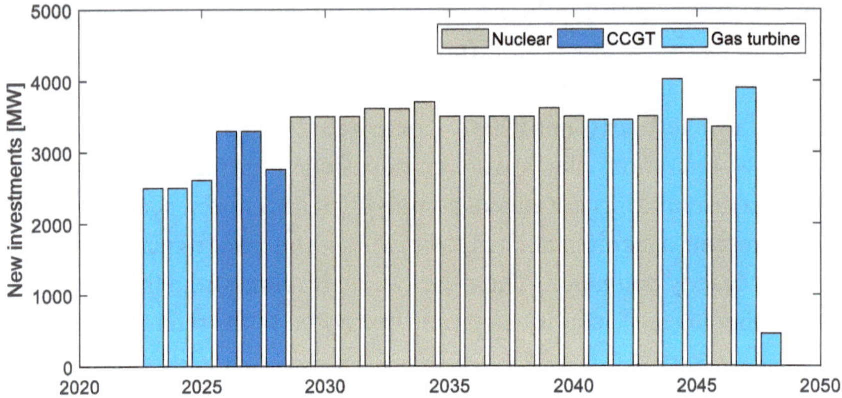

Figure 24: New investments in the SoS+ case.

Conclusively, it can be stated that the SoS+ case leads to higher overall capacity payments, but provides a higher installed capacity and thus a higher security of supply level. Further, it can be concluded, that the developed simulation model is able to produce feasible and expectable results, when the parameter values are changed.

5.3. SoS- Case

The third case that is considered in the result chapter, is the SoS- case. The SoS- case was created to assess the impact of a lower security factor combined with a larger amount of demand response measures available in the electricity price forecast. The lower security factor leads to a lower overall capacity obligation for the demand side. The increased amount of demand response measures however leads to a decrease of the forecasted price levels, as less hours reaching the price cap are obtained. This collusion leads to the capacity price development shown in Figure 25 and the investments provided by Figure 26.

Resulting from the rarer appearance of price caps in the electricity price forecast of the first years, the difference costs of the power plants increase compared to the previous cases, and therefore the capacity prices in the auctions until 2023. After 2023, the capacity prices rise strongly and reach the price caps for several consecutive years until 2031. The interpretation for the effect is provided in the interpretation of the reference case and can be applied to the SoS- case, too. However, compared to the reference case and the SoS+ case, where the high-price period lasts until 2034 and 2035 respectively, this period is shorter in the SoS- case. From 2032 on, the prices are on a level close to zero and only start rising again from 2047 on.

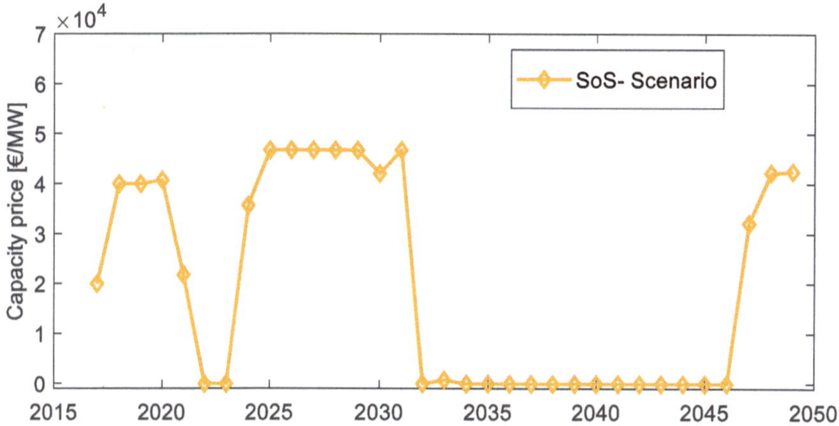

Figure 25: Capacity price development in the SoS- case.

The structure of the investments is, like in the other two cases, strongly influenced by the assumed decommissioning of the nuclear power plants. Despite showing the same general pattern as in the two previous cases, the impact of the lower capacity obligation and the change in the electricity price forecasts is visible taking a closer look at the results. Resulting from a lower expected profitability of the investment options and the lower capacity obligation, the investment decisions in the first years lead to a different plant park development. Considering only the investments until 2028 like in the previous chapters, in the SoS- case as well only gas-fired power plants are commissioned in the period from 2023 to 2028. However, compared to the 14.4 GW of the reference case and the 17.0 GW of the

SoS+ case, in the SoS- case only 11.9 GW new gas-fired power plants are added, complying with a difference of 2.5 GW compared to the reference case and 5.1 GW compared to the SoS+ case.

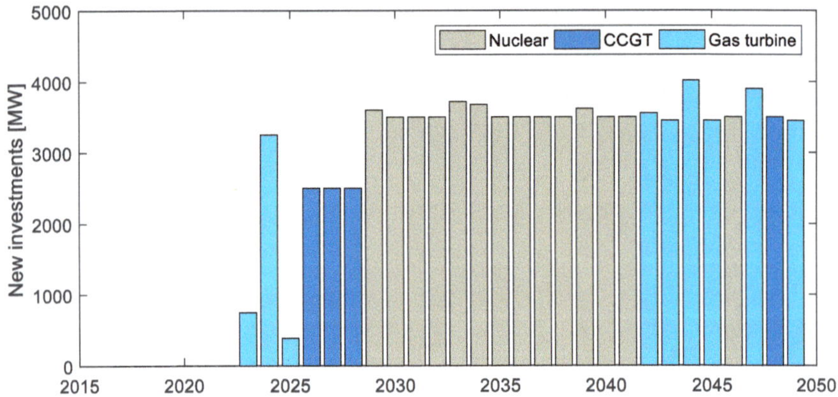

Figure 26: New investments in the SoS- case.

In can thus be concluded, that the reduced security factor and thus the reduced capacity obligation lead to less investments. The increased demand response volume considered in the price forecasts enhances this tendency. As a results, the installed capacity is lower compared to the other cases, complying with a lower level of security of supply. In the scope of this work it was not analysed, to which extent the electricity system obtained in the SoS- case can compete with the reference case and the SoS+ case in terms of security of supply, but as a lower total capacity is installed, the LOLE is likely to be higher than in the previous cases.

The overall capacity payments however are not significantly lower compared to the reference case and amount to 43 billion € until 2050. The key driver for that is the increased capacity price level in the first years, which is caused by lower expected power plant incomes from the energy market as a consequence of a larger amount of demand response measures considered. Note, that demand response measures are not respected in the capacity auctions in the simulation model, but only influence the presented results through the electricity price forecasts.

6. Critical Reflection and Outlook

This chapter discusses the shortcomings of the developed model and identifies improvements that may be considered in a further development of the model. It contains six issues that were identified by the developer: The determination of feasible mechanism parameters, the evaluation of the security of supply, a demand adaption following from the capacity mechanism, the missing cross-border participation, the consideration of nuclear shutdowns and investments and finally a missing strategy diversification of the agents. One by one, these issues are discussed in the following.

6.1. Determination of Mechanism Parameters

The parameters of the capacity mechanism have to be determined carefully. Naturally, an implemented capacity remuneration mechanism does not inevitably result in an adequate remuneration of capacities, but has to be reviewed constantly to obtain a feasible and cost-efficient parameter configuration. As the RTE in the real world will adapt mechanism parameters to the changing electricity system if necessary, the changing electricity system in the simulation as well may require an adaption of parameters.

For example, there is the case in which the capacities of individual technologies are granted too many capacity certificates, according to an overestimation of the contribution of the capacities to reducing the shortfall risk in peak load periods. A surplus of capacity certificates leads to capacity prices on a lower level, despite having an actual capacity shortage in the electricity system. The shortage can be detected by consulting the electricity price forecasts. If the electricity price forecast contains a large number of hours with scarcity and is thus reaching the price cap frequently, the capacity market is malfunctioning due to a poor calibration of the parameters. The described situation resembles the situation of an energy only market, because investments are incentivized not by the capacity remuneration mechanism but by extreme prices on the electricity market, which are occurring with a strong uncertainty. The implemented French capacity mechanism confronts this problem by an ex-post evaluation of the contribution of certified capacities after the delivery period. By means of this, the level of certification is adjusted to the effective contribution and a difference between certified capacity and effective capacity is identified. However, considering the time lag between the capacity auctions and the ex-post evaluation of the actual contribution, the mechanism is distorted in any case. The simulation model does not consider any ex-post evaluation and thus the capacity credits for each technology remain constant over the simulation period.

Another example for a bad calibration can be construed considering the parameter security factor. The security factor represents the contribution of neighbouring countries and cross-border electricity exchanges in counteracting the shortfall risk. In consequence, the French electricity system does not need to be able to satisfy the peak demand on its own by certified capacity, but can rely on imports from neighbouring countries in scarcity situations. The expected peak demand gets multiplied with the security factor in order to determine the capacity obligation for the demand side. As the peak demand is an essential and large factor of the capacity mechanism and the security factor is the proportional relation the capacity obligation, even a slight change of the security factor can lead to a considerable malfunctioning of the capacity mechanism. Considering a peak demand of roughly 100 GW, a change of the security factor by only one percent would result in a change of the capacity market volume of 1 GW. In contrast to the level of capacity certification, that relies on several different parameters and is carried out for each technology separately, the security factor consists of only one figure and is fixed for the entire mechanism. Thus, the mechanism functioning is very vulnerable to a bad choice of the security factor. An overestimation of the security factor would result in an underestimation of the level of security of supply and thus lead to an unnecessarily large capacity obligation. In the long-term, this could result in costly overcapacity. On the other hand, if the security factor is underestimated, there is a situation similar to the case where capacities are granted too many certificate and the capacity market does not reflect a critical generation adequacy. Even if the prices for capacity certificates are on a low level, there are situations of critical scarcity and resulting high prices on the electricity markets. A capacity mechanism with an underestimated security factor may not provide the desired investment incentives and have similar characteristics as the energy-only market.

Thus, in the course of modelling and simulating the French capacity market using the model of the present work, the parameters were checked carefully and need to be checked carefully in a possible further development of the model. It is not self-evident to assume the parameter values for the actual capacity mechanism provided by RTE to be the parameter values suiting the best for the capacity market model developed in the present work. In the procedure of modelling, some aspects of the actual capacity mechanism design have been treated differently or have been abstracted. Thus, the optimal values of the parameters might be slightly different from the values RTE determined to be the best-suiting for the capacity mechanism in reality. This applies less for the level of capacity certification, but more for the security factor.

In this context, it may be useful to develop a dynamic parametrisation approach for the simulation model. Based on the results in the capacity market and the electricity market and on the observed level of security of supply, the security factor could be adapted endogenously by the market operator agent each period of time, e.g. each ten years. Like that, the opportunity to change the parameter values in the real world and the assessment of the security of supply could be integrated in the simulation model.

In the end, there is no certainty, that the defined parameter values are the best suiting to the simulation model. For that purpose, sensitivities were analysed in the previous chapter to investigate the interrelation between the security factor and the model results. However, these are just the quantitative results of the simulation model and do not contain an evaluation of the realised security of supply level. To be able to draw sophisticated conclusions regarding the security of supply, the model needs to be further developed. The following section addresses this issue.

6.2. Security of Supply Evaluation

As was seen in the regulatory framework and the studies presented in section 4.5, the French security of supply target is defined by the loss of load expectation (LOLE). The LOLE is determined by applying the power plant park to a Monte Carlo simulation, in which multiple weather and power plant outage scenarios are simulated. Throughout all scenarios, the average number of hours with loss of load shall not exceed three, complying with a LOLE of three hours.

In the developed simulation model, the realised security of supply level is not evaluated ex post, but only enters the simulation ex ante through the security factor. A higher security factor complies with a higher capacity obligation and thus with a higher expected security of supply target. However, it must be analysed in the further development of the model, how to evaluate the security of supply level of the obtained power system and to which extent the security of supply targets are met. In the end, it is not sufficient to meet the capacity obligation to state the security of supply target is met, but the LOLE of the obtained electricity system must be analysed and quantified.

6.3. Demand Adaption

One of the objectives of the French capacity mechanism is to provide investment incentives to both the supply and the demand side, as a more flexible demand side can equally reduce the shortfall risk. In the current PowerACE model however, a "demand response" investment option is not implemented and the capacity obligation is given by the peak demand exogenously. In the model logic, the obligated parties are price-taking and therefore it must be guaranteed that the entire exogenously given certificate demand is satisfied. As a result, the demand curve on the capacity market is price-inelastic and the price level is only determined by the supply bids. The model thus neglects a demand adjustment, which may in the real world be economically more reasonable than the expansion of the power plant park.

In the real-world mechanism, demand response can be marketed implicitly, i.e. through the reduction of the obligation of a obligated party, and explicitly, i.e. in the capacity auctions. A further development of the simulation model should attempt to define a "demand response" investment option, in which investment planners can invest. The option complies with demand response measures that can be deployed at a certain price and is limited in amount by the technical potential in France. If the demand response option is chosen, demand response capacity is added to electricity system and the investor is granted capacity certificates, which he can explicitly market through the capacity auction. However, the investment in demand response measures requires a different investment appraisal than investments in new generation units. Further, demand response measures are difficult to integrate in the PowerACE plant dispatch logic. For these reasons, the implementation was left to a possible further development of the capacity mechanism model.

The deployment of a demand response option would indeed lead to a more flexible demand curve, both on the electricity market and on the capacity market. In that sense, with the demand response option the desired investment incentives for a demand adaption could be respected and the model would depict an important facet of the mechanism that was so far neglected.

6.4. Cross-Border Participation and Market Coupling

The market area that is considered in the capacity mechanism model by now, contains only France. Electricity exchanges are considered by time series, based on historical electricity exchanges. However, France is part of the European Internal Market and thus the electricity exchange is the result of a market procedure, if the transmission capacities are not fully used. In addition, from 2019 on foreign capacities will be allowed to participate in the French capacity market, if they can prove sufficient transmission capacity.

PowerACE has already implemented market coupling and the European electricity markets are depicted, so in a next step the model should be extended and include coupled markets and foreign participation in order to get a more detailed view on the interdependencies with the neighbouring countries in the European Internal Market. However, in the scope of this work this could not be respected.

Regarding the cross-border participation in the capacity mechanism, no substantial changes can be expected, as the available transfer capacity is a strong limitation. Thus, only a small amount of foreign capacity is expected be able to participate in the capacity market, if not none. As discussed in section 3.3, the transfer capacity is already used economically and it therefore remains to be seen, if the participation in the French capacity mechanism will be economically competitive to the current use.

6.5. Nuclear Power Plants

One of the biggest shortcomings of the developed model is the consideration of nuclear power plants. First, the shutdown of old power plants is given by the technical lifetime approach. This approach leads to a rapid and uncoordinated shutdown of nuclear power plants between 2026 and 2042, that is not expectable from the real world development. To the simulation model, it complies with a severe exogenously introduced scarcity and results in the dynamics explained in 5.1. However, to depict the decommissioning of the nuclear fleet more realistically a different approach might be pursued, to obtain a smoother and even market exit. For example, applying a uniformly distributed decommission over a certain period of time. This may mitigate the extent of the decommissioning impact on the system development.

Second, the investments in new nuclear power or overhauls of old plant will most likely not take place only on market basis, but will be triggered politically. Since nuclear power contributes to such a large share to the French electricity generation, it is unlikely that new investments will be left to the free market by the French government. Further, EDF as a company dominates the French market, which makes strategic behaviour likely when it comes to such a substantial question. However, this development is hardly predictable, therefore no premature assumptions should be introduced to the model.

But even the assumption of a politically led integrated[14] nuclear generation change leads to consequences for the simulation results, the logic is as follows: The politically triggered shutdowns and new investments enter the system exogenously and lead to a different expectation about future scarcity, as there is sufficient investment security for EDF and no competition-based investment appraisal is required. This leads to a reduction of the electricity price forecast level and thus to a changed investment behaviour. The changed expectations also have an impact on the capacity prices, as they are based on the electricity price forecast. As a consequence to the exogenous shutdowns and new investments, less investment takes place based on the weakened market incentives, thus the overcapacity in the years 2026 to 2031, that was identified in the reference case (see chapter 5.1), may be reduced. The consequences for the capacity market are then lower difference costs for the requested capacity in the considered period and consequently a more moderate capacity price level. Introducing an integrated policy-driven nuclear generation change could thus lead to a lower

[14] Integrated in the sense, that shutdowns and new investments are coordinated and do not take place independently based on the market logic.

and more constant capacity price level, but would also distort the functioning and logic of the liberalised market. The issue that arises at this point is the conflict between the functioning of a liberalised market and system planning by a central planner. The political integrated solution would certainly be oriented at the cost-effective solution and aim to generate a cost-effective generation system. However, in the presence of an exogenous influence, the market logic does not provide the same incentive structure.

For the scope of the work it is sufficient to be aware of the shortcoming and to reflect the impact of a possible policy intervention on the results. The uncertainty about future policy measures cannot be captured by a simulation model, thus the future development remains to be seen.

6.6. Diversification of Bidding Strategies

The last shortcoming of the model that shall be discussed in this chapter, addresses the diversification of the capacity market bidding strategies. As previously outlined, the structure of the capacity market model allows to diversify the behaviour of the different players involved in the capacity market. It is unlikely to observe the same bidding strategy based on difference costs by all market players in the real-world capacity auctions.

A thorough game-theoretic analysis of different bidding strategies for different market players is necessary to obtain feasible and diversified bidding strategies. In the scope of this work, such an analysis was not possible and is thus left to future works and a further development of the model. A significant potential strength of the approach developed in this work is therefore not realised yet. The lack of agent-based character in the model must be criticised in the current state, as the model is just a system dynamics simulation model without strategy diversification.

Possible bidding strategies can for example contain average difference costs considering more than one year, or take into account further cost components. Particularly in the case of old nuclear power plants, it is easily imaginable to include expected deconstruction costs in the capacity bid or to build financial reserves for future investments by additional capacity revenues. Even though it is not the objective of the capacity mechanism to finance the costly deconstruction and replacement of old nuclear power plants, it may be a bidding strategy of the nuclear power plant owner to generate revenues exceeding the difference costs of the considered year. In any case it is unlikely, that the capacity bids in reality will decrease to a price of zero. Market participants have no incentive to let the price drop to zero. On the one hand because a market clearing price of zero results in no additional revenue in the short term. On the other hand and more significant, because capacity prices of zero indicate that the capacity mechanism is obsolete. No capacity owner has the incentive to indicate, that the mechanism is obsolete, because it serves as a desirable source of additional income, independent from if it is required to operate profitably or not.

It can thus be concluded, that more attention should be paid on how capacity bids are generated in a further development of the capacity mechanism model, because the difference costs approach does not sufficiently reflect the bidding strategy of all market participants. A diversification of strategies would exploit the potential of the agent-based structure and lead to more sophisticated simulation results.

7. Conclusions

In the closing chapter, the master thesis and the main conclusions drawn from the analysis and the simulation results are summarised. As was seen in chapter 2, the French electricity system underwent a substantial change in the past years that is still ongoing. The main characteristics of this change are an increasing and more volatile peak load and a lack of flexible demand or peak generation capacity to cover these load peaks in extreme weather events. As a reaction to the threat to the security of supply, the French government implemented a decentralised capacity remuneration mechanism. All consumption is obliged to buy capacity certificates appropriate to their expected load in peak periods, whereas all generation capacities and demand response measures are granted capacity certificates in amount of their contribution in peak periods. The certificate price is determined in capacity auctions that take place prior to the respective delivery year. This additional source of income shall guarantee the profitability of existing generation units and provide incentives for investments in new peak generation units and flexibility on the demand side. Thus, the mechanism shall eventually lead to guaranteeing the security of supply of the French electricity system.

The further development of the simulation model and the discussion of alternative approaches to analyse impacts of the French capacity mechanism provided valuable insights to the functioning and possible vulnerabilities of the mechanism. The key parameters that were identified are the security factor, the capacity credits of each technology and the consideration of demand response capacities in the electricity price forecast.

In the results chapter, the simulation results of three different cases were analysed and interpreted. Hereby, both the interdependencies of the identified key simulation parameters were investigated and the development of the French generation park and the capacity prices were addressed. Depending on the parameter setting, different new investments and security of supply levels were observed. In the reference case, a total of 14.4 GW of gas-fired power plants are commissioned until 2028, whereas in the SoS- case and the SoS+ case the investments in gas-fired power plants in the same period amount to 11.9 GW and 17.0 GW, respectively. The capacity prices in all cases show a similar pattern, but in a thorough analysis differences between the defined cases were identified and explained. However, the exogenous shutdown of nuclear generation capacity in the years 2026 till 2042 is an essential driver for the long-term capacity price development in the simulation model. In further research, the generation change in nuclear energy may be considered in a different way.

The research questions[15] of this master thesis can be answered now. The French capacity mechanism as a complement to the electricity markets is able to provide appropriate investment incentives to new peak generation units. Depending on the parameter setting, different levels of security of supply can be realised. The capacity mechanism is thus effective and controllable. The impact on the evolution of the French generation park was assessed in-depth in the results chapter. In the mid-term, investments in new gas-fired power plants are incentivised. The extent of these investments depends mainly on the security factor and the consequent capacity obligation for the demand side. However, even in presence of a capacity mechanism, the expected revenues from electricity sales remain the essential decision factor in the investment appraisal. In particular in the long-term, investment decisions are taken even without additional capacity revenue expectations, as the expected rapid shutdown of nuclear generation capacity creates an imminent scarcity and thus the electricity price forecasts are increased.

It is arguable, whether the generation change of nuclear power will take

[15] Research questions as defined in introduction: Is the French capacity mechanism able to guarantee the security of supply? What is its impact on the evolution of the French power generation park?

place on a market basis alone, or if a policy-driven solution will be consulted. In the simulation model developed in this work, the generation change is accompanied by a period of very high capacity prices, leading to a large financial burden for the demand side. Assuming the reaching of the price cap, in one delivery year the payments can amount to up to 4.6 billion €, complying with roughly 1 Cent per consumed kWh.

The question that arises is therefore, whether the capacity mechanism is required permanently or whether it may be more feasible to abandon it before the changes in the nuclear generation fleet are imminent. As Keppler (2017) observed, capacity remuneration mechanisms tend to make themselves obsolete over time. This conclusion can also be drawn from the capacity price development obtained in the simulations and is indicated by the price drop after 2030. Thus, a fundamental revision of the capacity mechanism may be required in the future, at best coordinated with a possible nuclear energy policy.

Finally, it must be argued whether the capacity mechanism is a necessary measure in the French context. As was seen in chapter 2, the main threat to the security of supply is the temperature sensitivity of the load. From a German perspective, it is hardly understandable, that building heating causes such a substantial risk. However, policy measures subsidising heating efficiency, insulation in the building sector, heat storages or heating technologies other from electrical heating might as well be able to remedy the threat of the increasing and volatile peak load evolution.

In the end, the involved advisors and the French government considered the implementation of the capacity mechanism as the best of all options. However, as the capacity mechanism is market-wide, the entire generation fleet will gain extra revenues, which the energy sector will gladly accept. At the current capacity price level of 10,000 € per MWh, the certificates granted to the nuclear power plants alone will earn 550 million € per year. It must be argued, whether these additional revenues are appropriate or whether the capacity mechanism provides hidden subsidies to existing generation units, in particular the nuclear power plants operated by EDF.

To close this work, some final thoughts shall be conveyed. From an energy economics point of view, the implementation and design of a capacity mechanism is highly interesting as the paradigm of the benchmark model and the functioning of the energy-only market is challenged. Indeed, the electricity markets in reality contain some flaws compared to the theory of markets. As a consequence, a policy intervention might be necessary to provide the public good security of supply to the industry and to the people in France. Nevertheless, the risk of unnecessarily large costs for end consumers caused by bad mechanism calibration and the reservations on whether the additional revenues for the existing capacities are appropriate remain.

List of References

Bublitz, Andreas; Renz, Lea; Keles, Dogan; Genoese, Massimo and Fichtner, Wolf (2015): *"An assessment of the newly proposed strategic reserve in Germany." 12th International Conference on the European Energy Market (EEM 2015), Lissabon, 19-22 May 2015.*

CNP (2016): *"RTE: EDF, Caisse des Dépôts and CNP Assurances sign a binding agreement for a long-term partnership"*. Press release 16 December 2016, link: https://www.cnp.fr/en/Journalist/All-our-press-releases/2016/RTE-EDF-Caisse-des-Depots-and-CNP-Assurances-sign-a-binding-agreement-for-a-long-term-partnership#, *accessed: 2 May 2017.*

Cramton, Peter and Stoft, Steven (2006): *"The Convergence of Market Designs for Adequate Generating Capacity, with Special Attention to the CAISO's Resource Adequacy Problem."*, White Paper for the Electricity Oversight Board.

De Vries, Laurens and Heijnen, Petra (2008): *"The impact of electricity market design upon investment under uncertainty: the effectiveness of capacity mechanisms." Utilities Policy 16 (3)*, 215–227.

EC (2016): *"Commission Decision of 8.11.2016 on state aid scheme SA.39621 2015/C (ex 2015/NN)."* European Commission, Brussels.

EC (2011): *"Energy Roadmap 2050"*, European Commission.

EDF (2017): *"Répartition du capital social au 30 mars 2017"* link: www.edf.fr/groupe-edf/espaces-dedies/finance/informationsfinancieres/l-action-edf/structure-du-capital, *accessed: 2 May 2017.*

ENTSO-E (2013): *"Scenario Outlook & Adequacy Forecast 2013-2030."*

EPEX Spot (2016): *"Aggregated demand and supply curve"* link: https://www.epexspot.com/fr/donnees_de_marche/capacitymarket/curve/capacity-agg-curve/2016-12-15/FR, *accessed: 2 May 2017.*

EPEX Spot (2017): *"Données de marché: Capacity Market."* link: https://www.epexspot.com/fr/donnees_de_marche/capacitymarket/curve/capacity-agg-curve/2017-04-27/FR, *accessed: 2 May 2017.*

Finon, Dominique and Pignon, Virginie (2008): *"Electricity and long-term capacity adequacy: The quest for regulatory mechanism compatible with electricity market." Utilities Policy 16 (3)*, 143-158.

Frontier Economics (2014): *"Impact Assessment of Capacity Mechanisms"*, Report for the Federal Ministry for Economic Affairs and Energy (BMWi).

FTI CL (2016): *"Assessment of the impact of the French capacity mechanism on electricity markets."* Paris.

Genoese, Massimo (2010): *„Energiewirtschaftliche Analysen des deutschen Strommarkts mit agentenbasierter Simulation."* Dissertation, Nomos Verlag Baden-Baden.

Genoese, Massimo; Genoese, Fabio and Fichtner, Wolf (2012): *"Model-based analysis of the impact of capacity markets on electricity markets." 9th International Conference on the European Energy Market (EEM 2012), Florence, 10-12 May 2012.*

Joskow, Paul L. (2008): *"Capacity payments in imperfect electricity markets: Need and design." Utilities Policy 16 (3)*, 159-170.

Keles, Dogan; Bublitz, Andreas; Zimmermann, Florian; Genoese, Massimo and Fichtner, Wolf (2016a): *"Analysis of design options for the electricity market: The German case." Applied Energy 183*, 884–901.

Keles, Dogan; Renz, Lea; Bublitz, Andreas; Zimmermann, Florian; Genoese, Massimo; Fichtner, Wolf; Höfling, Holger; Sensfuß, Frank and Winkler, Jenny (2016b): *"Zukunftsfähige Designoptionen für den deutschen Strommarkt: Ein Vergleich des Energy-only-Marktes mit Kapazitätsmärkten."* Karlsruhe. KIT Scientific Publishing.

Keppler, Jan Horst (2017): *"Rationales for capacity remuneration mechanisms: Security of supply externalities and asymmetric investment incentives." Energy Policy 105*, 562-570.

MEEM (2015): "*LOI n° 2015-992 du 17 août 2015 relative à la transition énergétique pour la croissance verte."* Ministère de l'Environnement, de l'Énergie et de la Mer (MEEM).

MEEM (2016): "*Mécanism de Capacité - Arrêté du 29 novembre 2016 définissant les règles du mécanisme de capacité et pris en application de l'article R. 335-2 du Code de l'énergie."* 29 November 2016. Ministère de l'Environnement, de l'Énergie et de la Mer (MEEM).

MEEM (2010): *"Plan d'action national en faveur des énergies renouvelables Période 2009-2020."* Ministère de l'Environnement, de l'Énergie et de la Mer (MEEM).

Ofgem (2014): *"Electricity Capacity Assessment Report 2014."* Office of Gas & Electricity Markets (Ofgem), UK Government.

Petitet, Marie (2016): *"Long-term dynamics of investment decisions in electricity markets with variable renewables development and adequacy objectives."* Dissertation, Paris, 29 November 2016.

Petitet, Marie; Finon, Dominique and Janssen, Tanguy (2017): *"Capacity adequacy in power markets facing energy transition: A comparison of scarcity pricing and capacity mechanism." Energy Policy 103*, 30–46.

Platts (2017): "*World Electric Power Plants Data Base" (WEPP).*

Poignant, Serge and Sido, Bruno (2010): *"La maîtrise de la pointe électrique."* Ministère de l'écologie, de l'énergie, du développement durable et de la mer (MEEM).

Renz, Lea; Keles, Dogan and Fichtner, Wolf (2014): *"Modellgestützte Analyse von Designoptionen für den deutschen Elektrizitätsmarkt zur Gewährleistung der Versorgungssicherheit bei zunehmender Stromerzeugung aus erneuerbaren Energien." 13. Symposium Energieinnovation (EnInnov 2014), Graz, 12-14 February 2014.*

Reuters (2016): "*French power cuts more likely after UK link outage - RTE.*" 1 December 2016, link: http://www.reuters.com/article/france-power-winteroutlook-idUSL8N1DW3O3, *accessed: 1 May 2017.*

Ringler, Philipp (2016): "*Erzeugungssicherheit und Wohlfahrt in gekoppelten Elektrizitätsmärkten*", Dissertation, Karlsruhe.

Ringler, Philipp; Bublitz, Andreas; Genoese, Massimo and Fichtner, Wolf (2014): *"A model-based analysis of generation adequacy in interconnected electricity markets." 11th International Conference on the European Energy Market (EEM14), Krakow 28-30 May 2014.*

RTE (2012): *"La vague de froid de février 2012."* Paris.

RTE (2014): *"French Capacity Market: Report accompanying the draft rules."* Paris.

RTE (2014): *"French Capacity Market: Report accompanying the draft rules."* Paris.

RTE (2017a): *"RTE d'hier à aujourd'hui."* link: http://www.rte-france.com/fr/article/rte-d-hier-aujourd-hui, *accessed: 2 May 2017.*

RTE (2017b): *"Bilan Prévisionnel de l'équilibre offre-demande d'électricité en France, Édition 2016."* Paris.

RTE (2017c): *Yearly Net Transfer Capacities.* link: https://clients.rte-france.com/lang/an/visiteurs/vie/ntc_annuelles.jsp?year=2016, accessed 22 May 2017.

RTE (2017d): *Website containing the published parameters: "Mécanisme de Capacité."* link: https://clients.rte-france.com/lang/fr/visiteurs/vie/meca_capa/meca_capa.jsp, *accessed: 2 May 2017.*

UFE and BDEW (2014): *"Energy transition and capacity mechanisms: A contribution to the European debate with a view to 2030."* Union Française de l'Électrité & Bundesverband deutsche Energie- und Wasserwirtschaft.

Vázquez, Carlos; Rivier, Michel and Pérez-Arriaga, Ignacio (2002): *"A Market Approach to Long-Term Security of Supply." IEEE Transactions on Power Systems 17 (2)*, 349-357.

Zimmermann, Florian; Bublitz, Andreas; Keles, Dogan; Dehler, Joris and Fichtner, Wolf (2016): *"An analysis of long-term impacts of demand response on investments in thermal power plants and generation adequacy." 13th International Conference on the European Energy Market (EEM), Porto, 6-9 June 2016.*

Zimmermann, Florian; Keles, Dogan and Wolf Fichtner (2017): *"Agentenbasierte Analyse der Auswirkungen des französischen Kapazitätsmarkts." 10. Internationale Energiewirtschaftstagung an der TU Wien (IEWT).*

FSC
www.fsc.org
MIX
Papier | Fördert gute Waldnutzung
FSC® C083411

Kolibri 360 GmbH
Ferdinand-Jühlke-Straße 7
99095 Erfurt, Deutschland
produktsicherheit@kolibri360.de